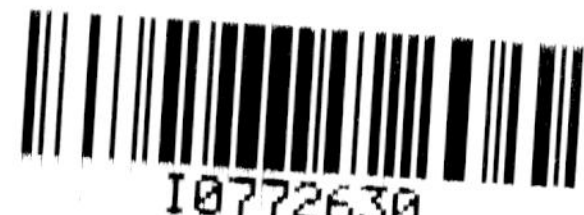

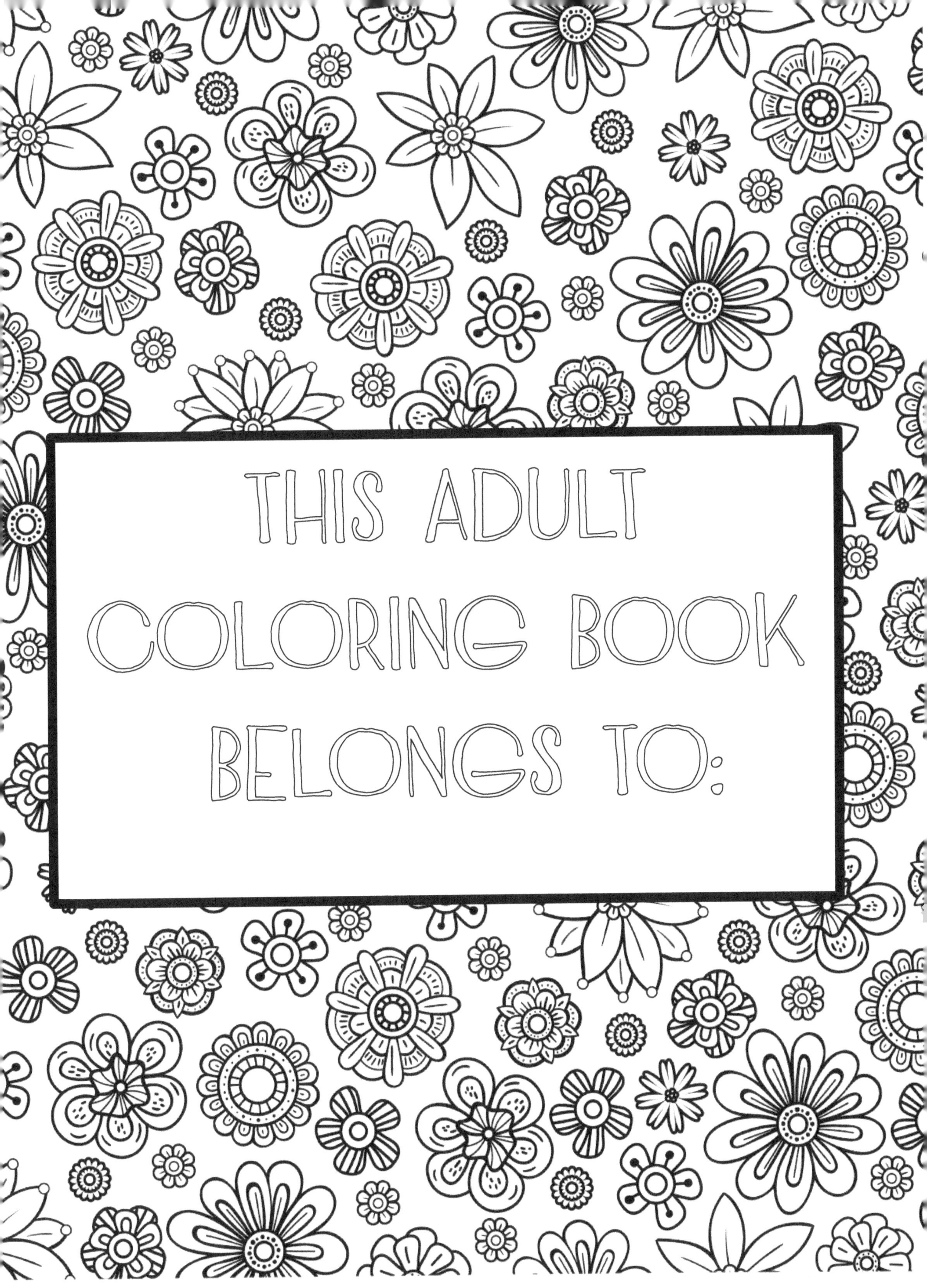

THIS ADULT
COLORING BOOK
BELONGS TO:

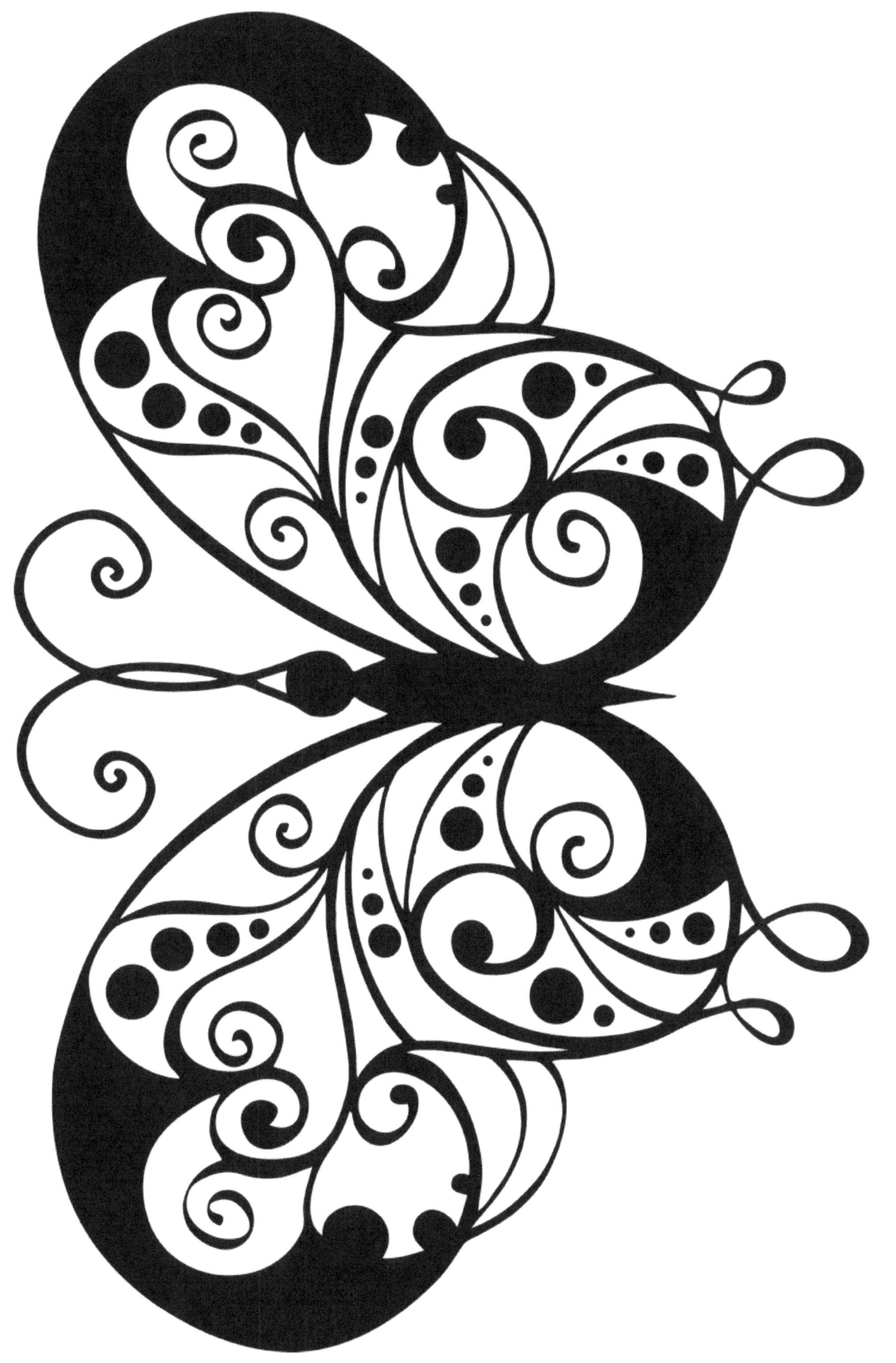

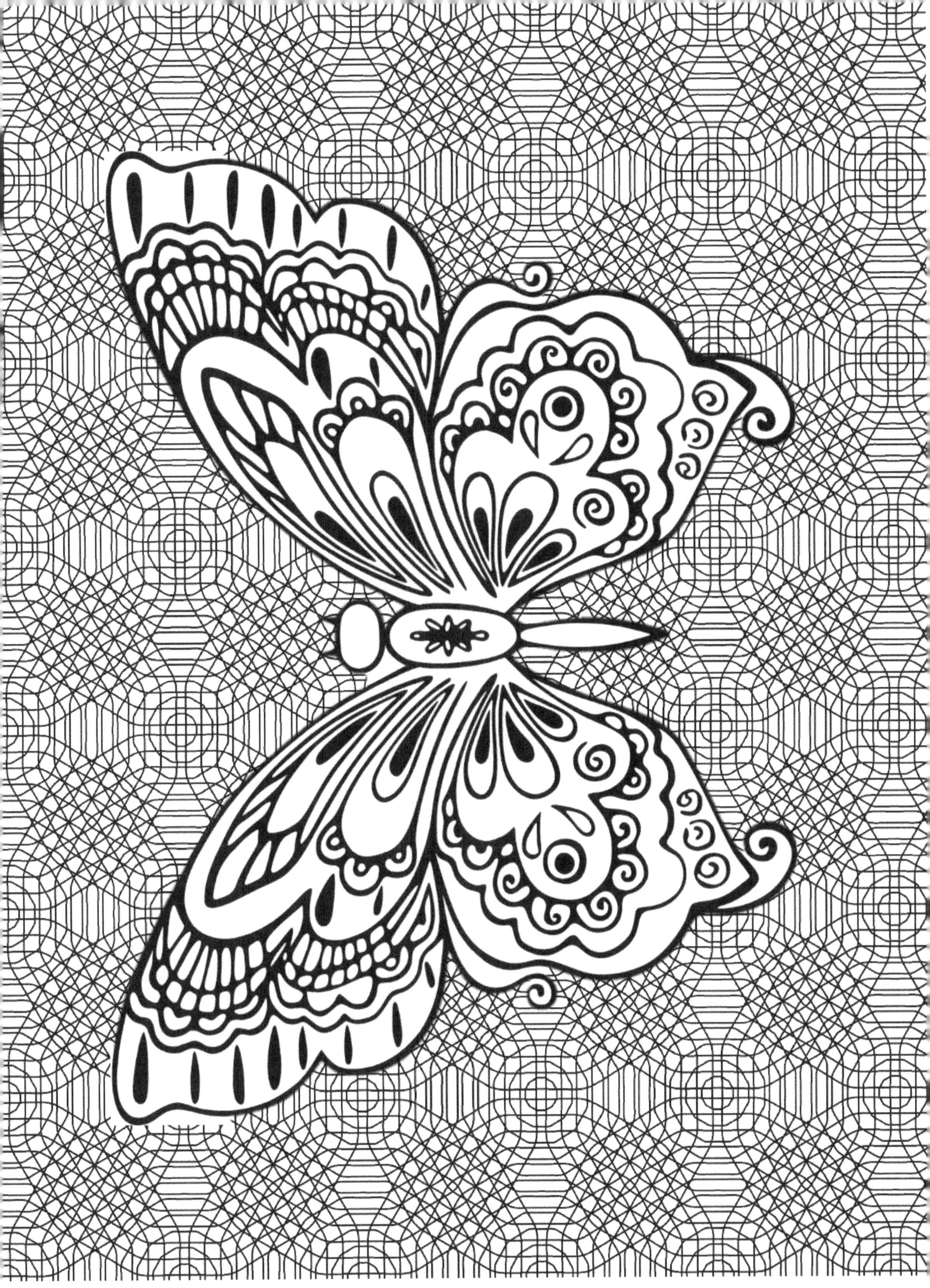

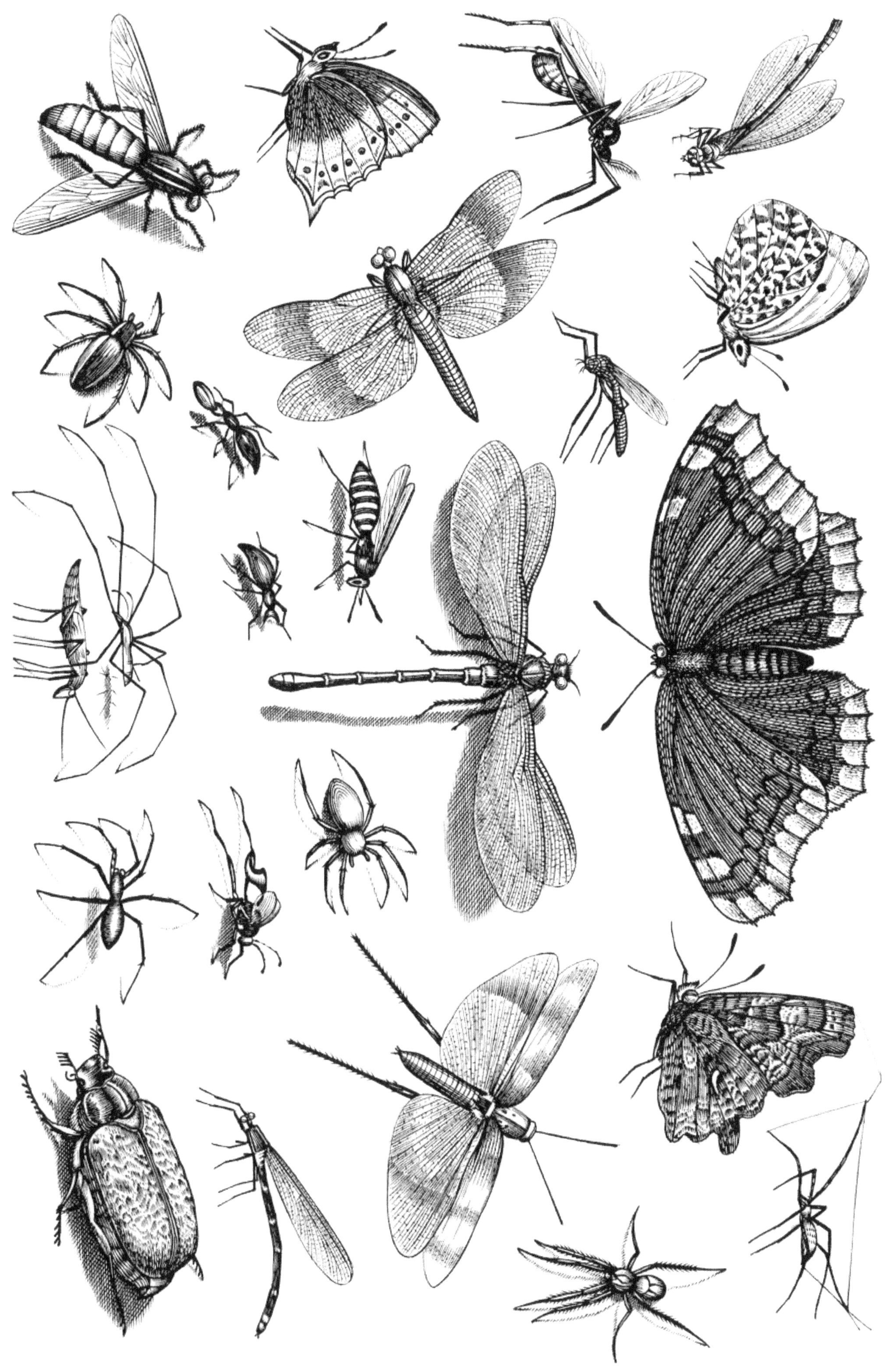

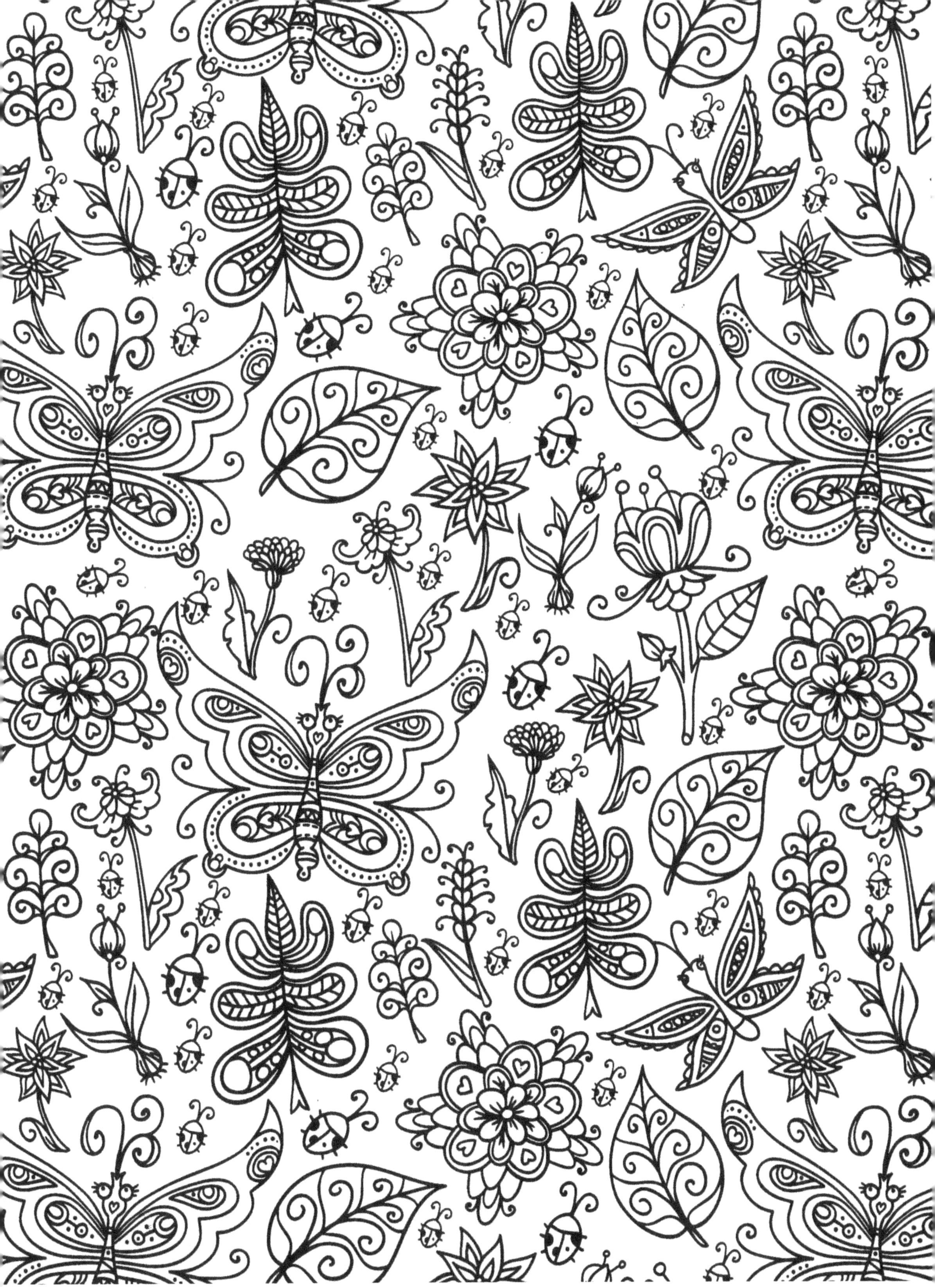

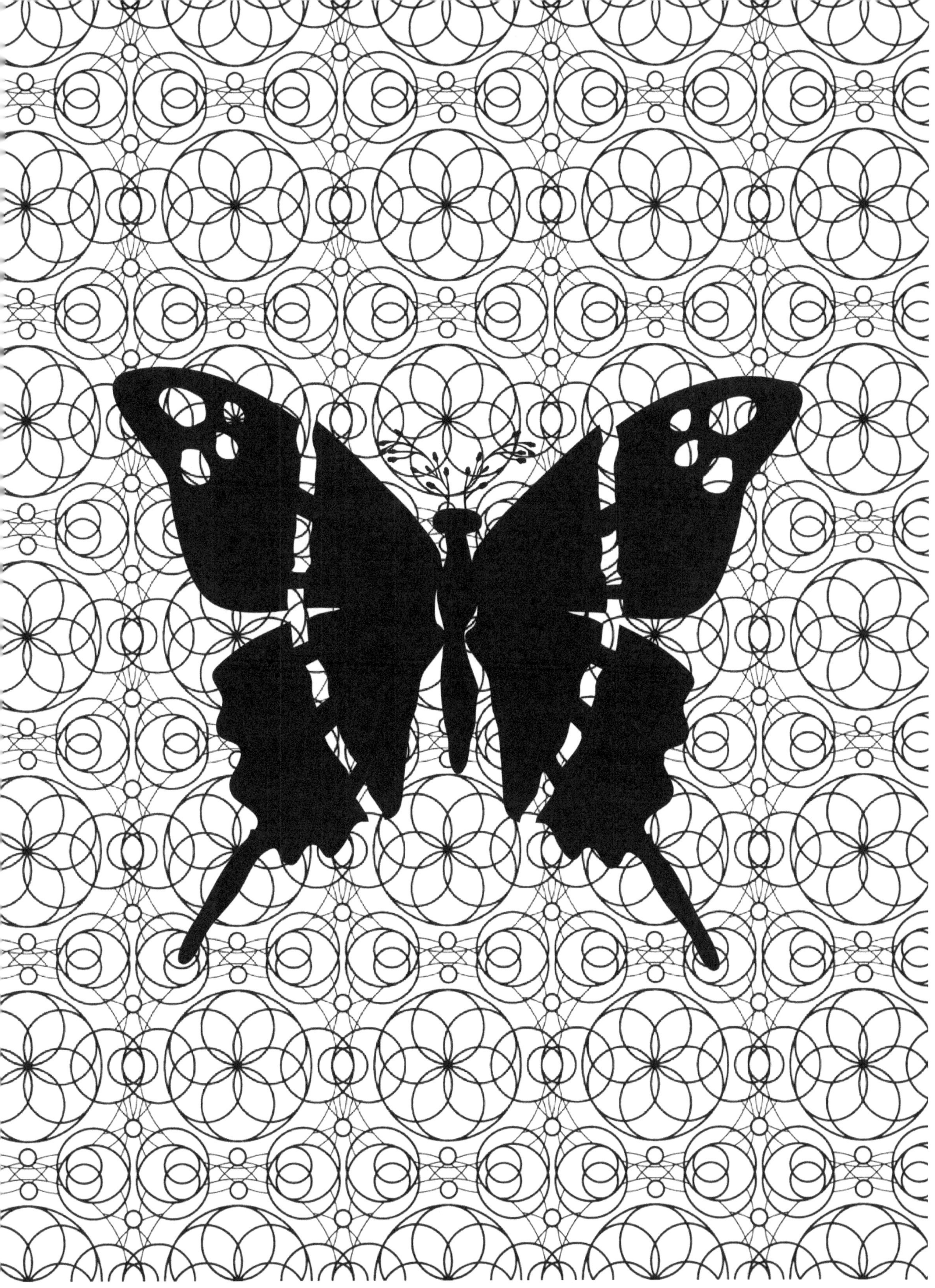

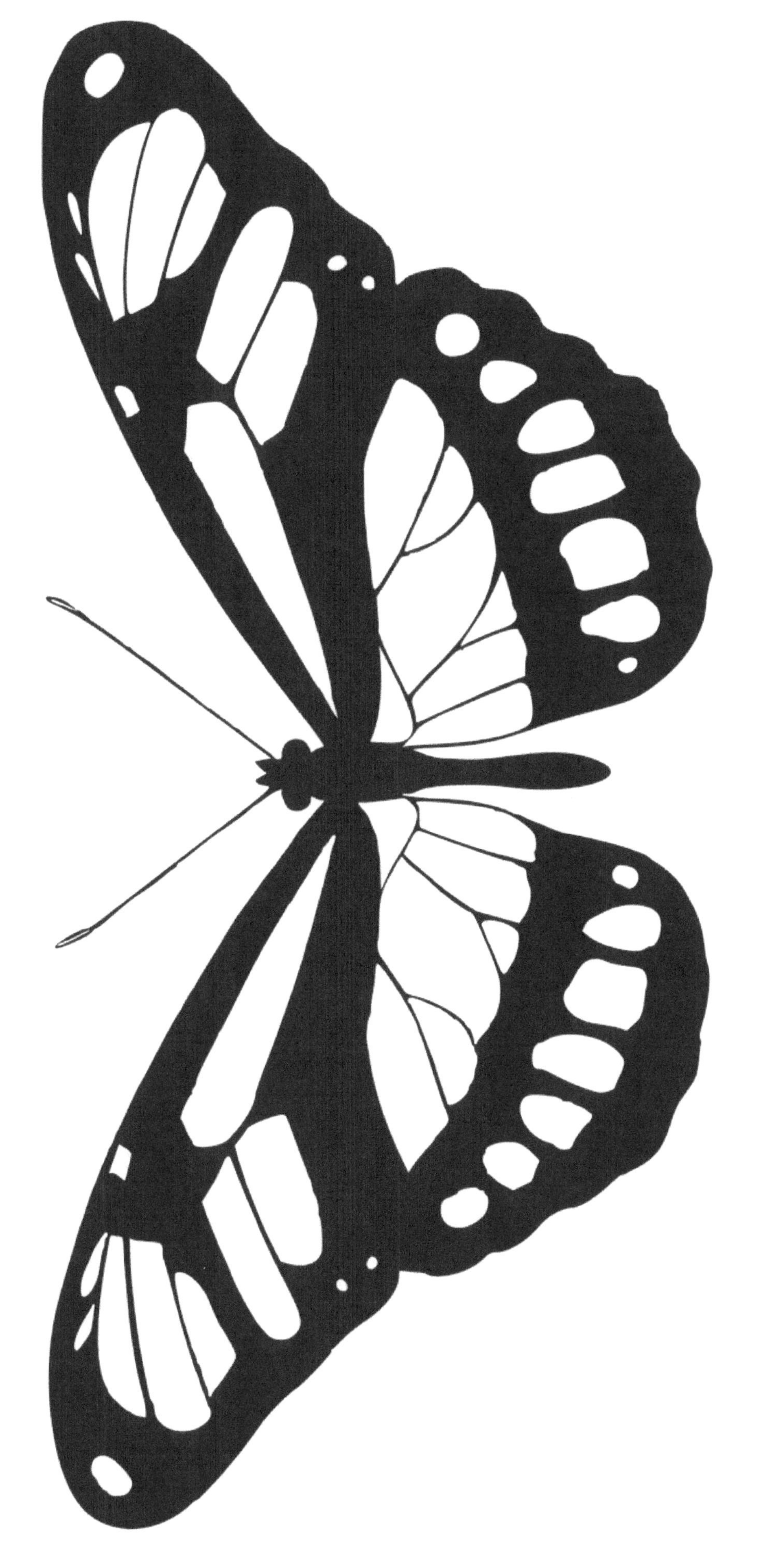

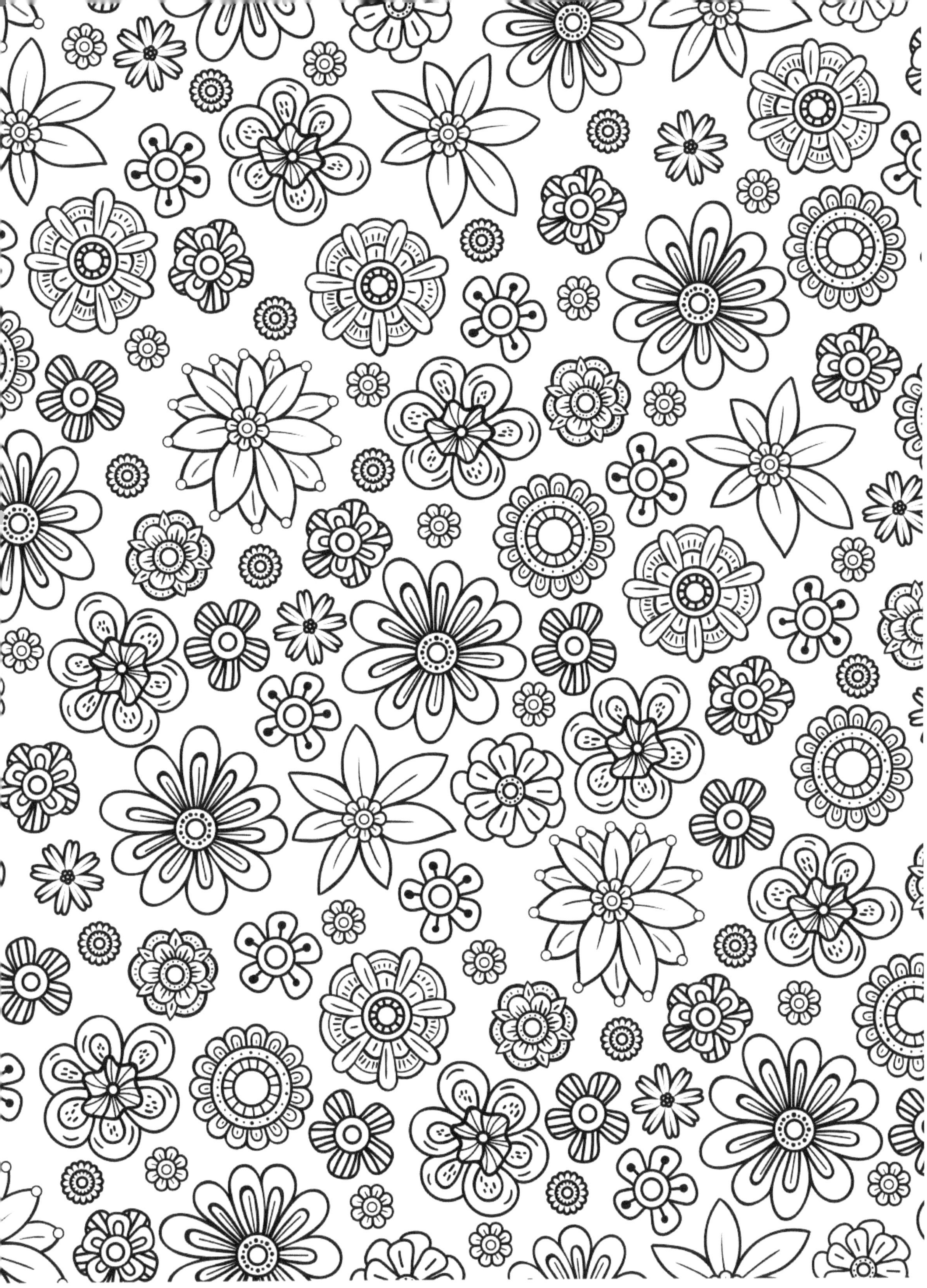

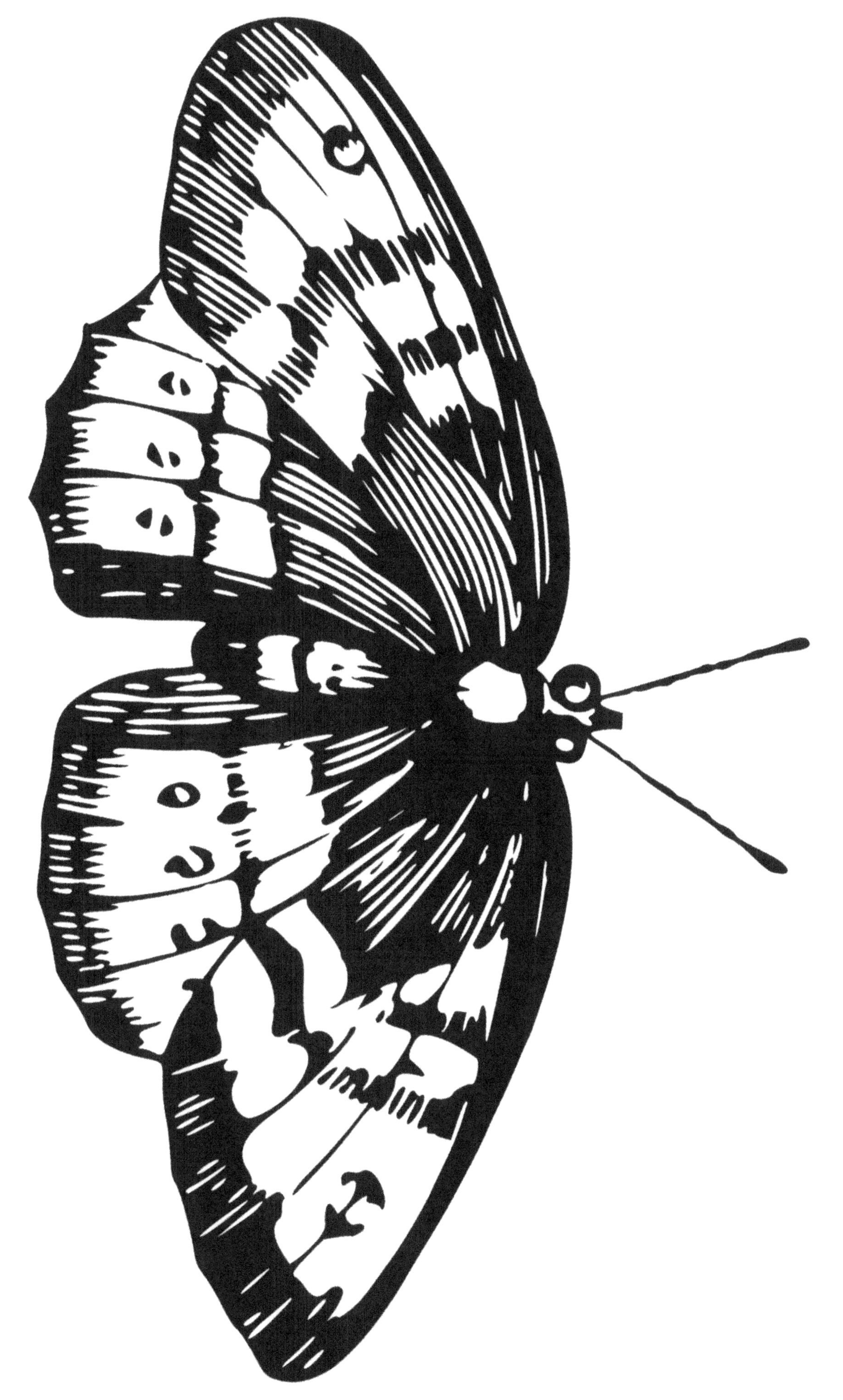

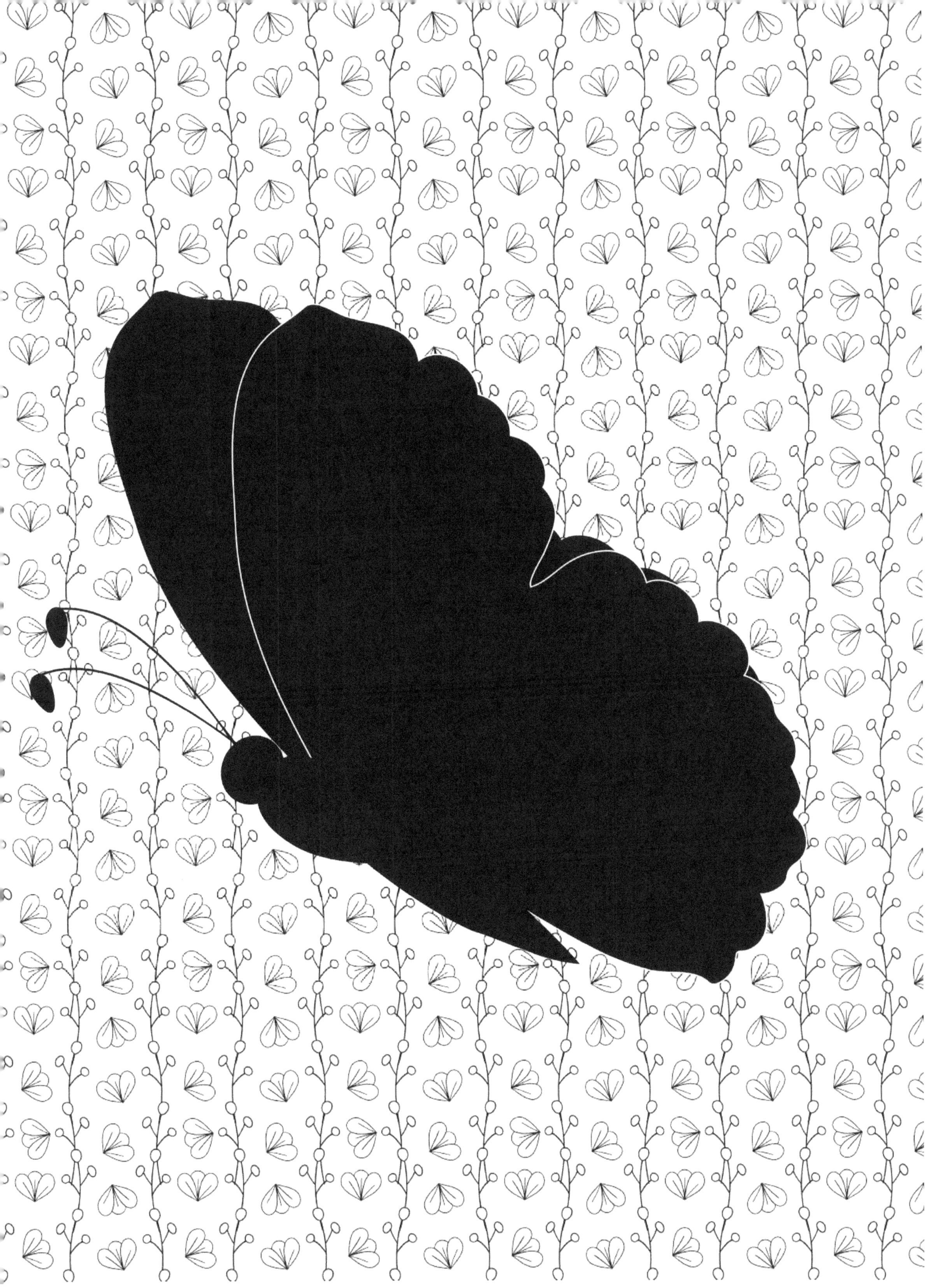

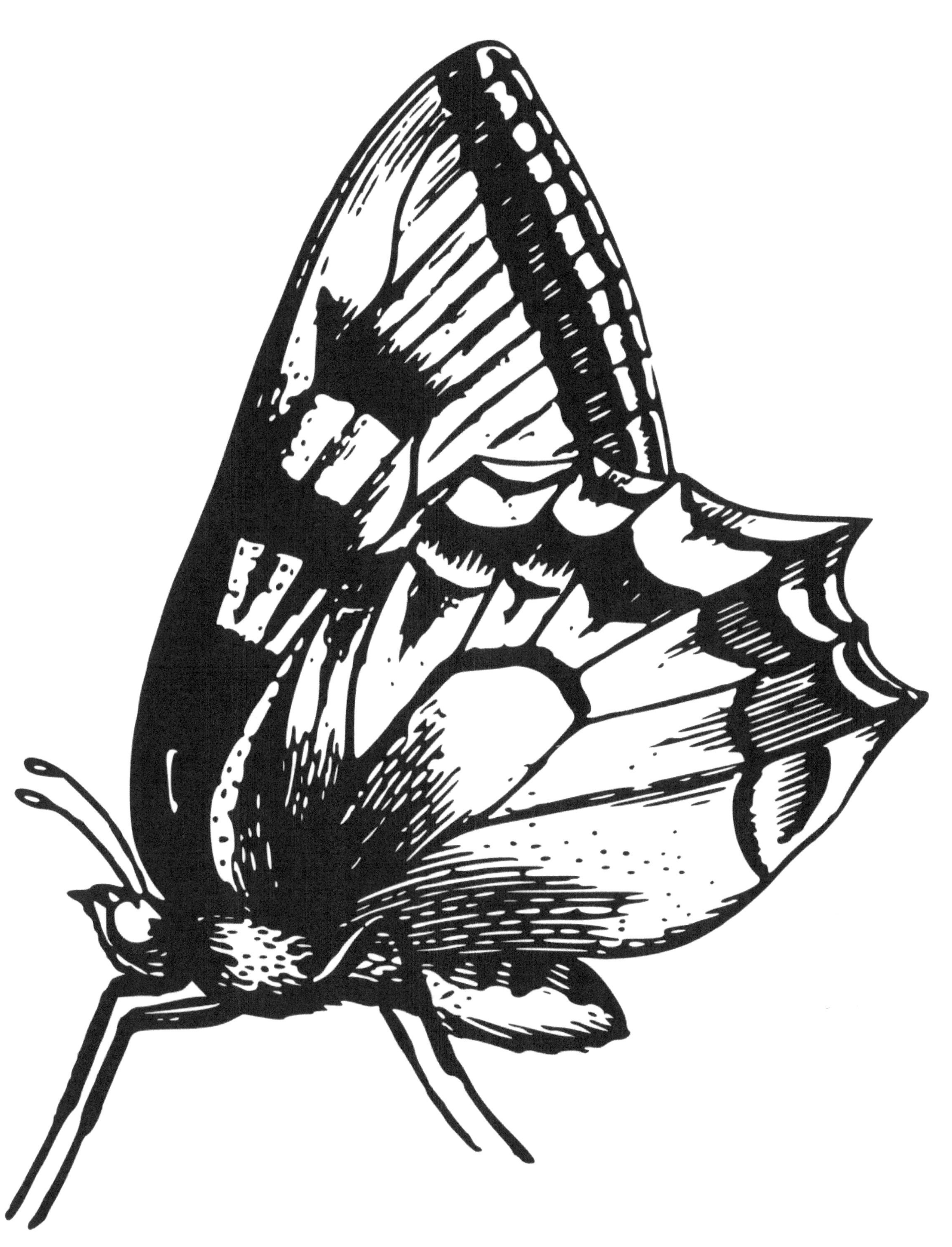

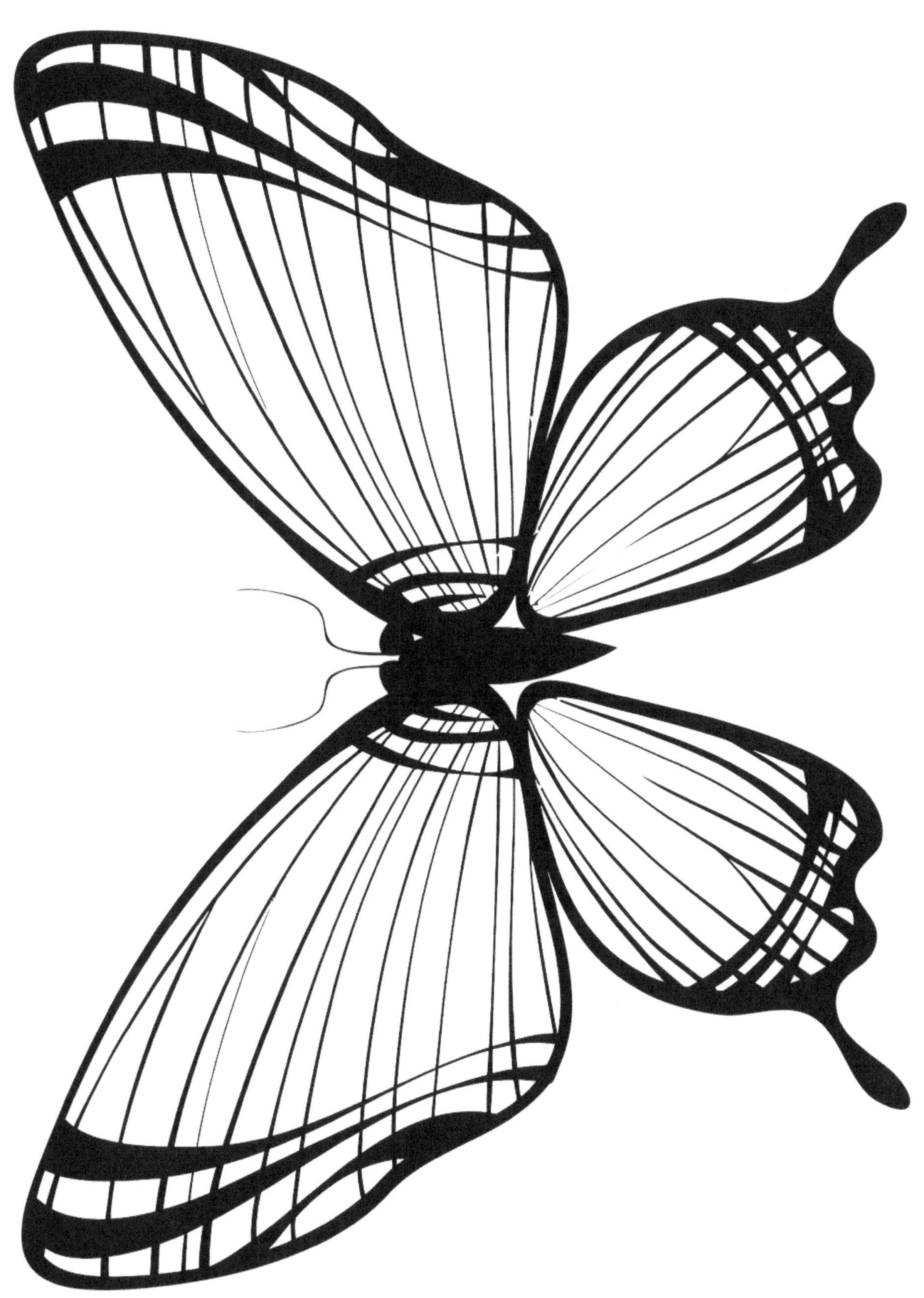

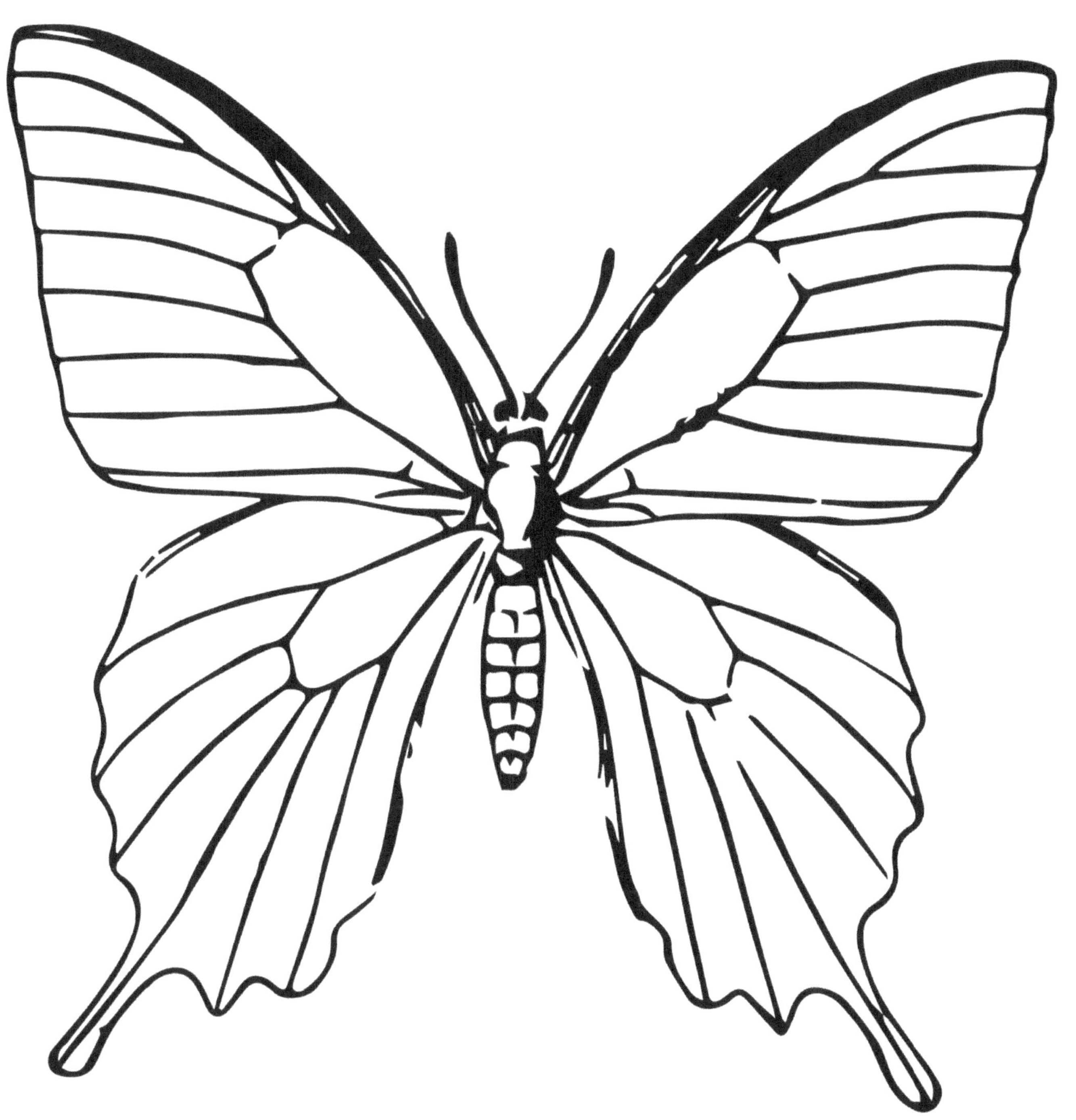

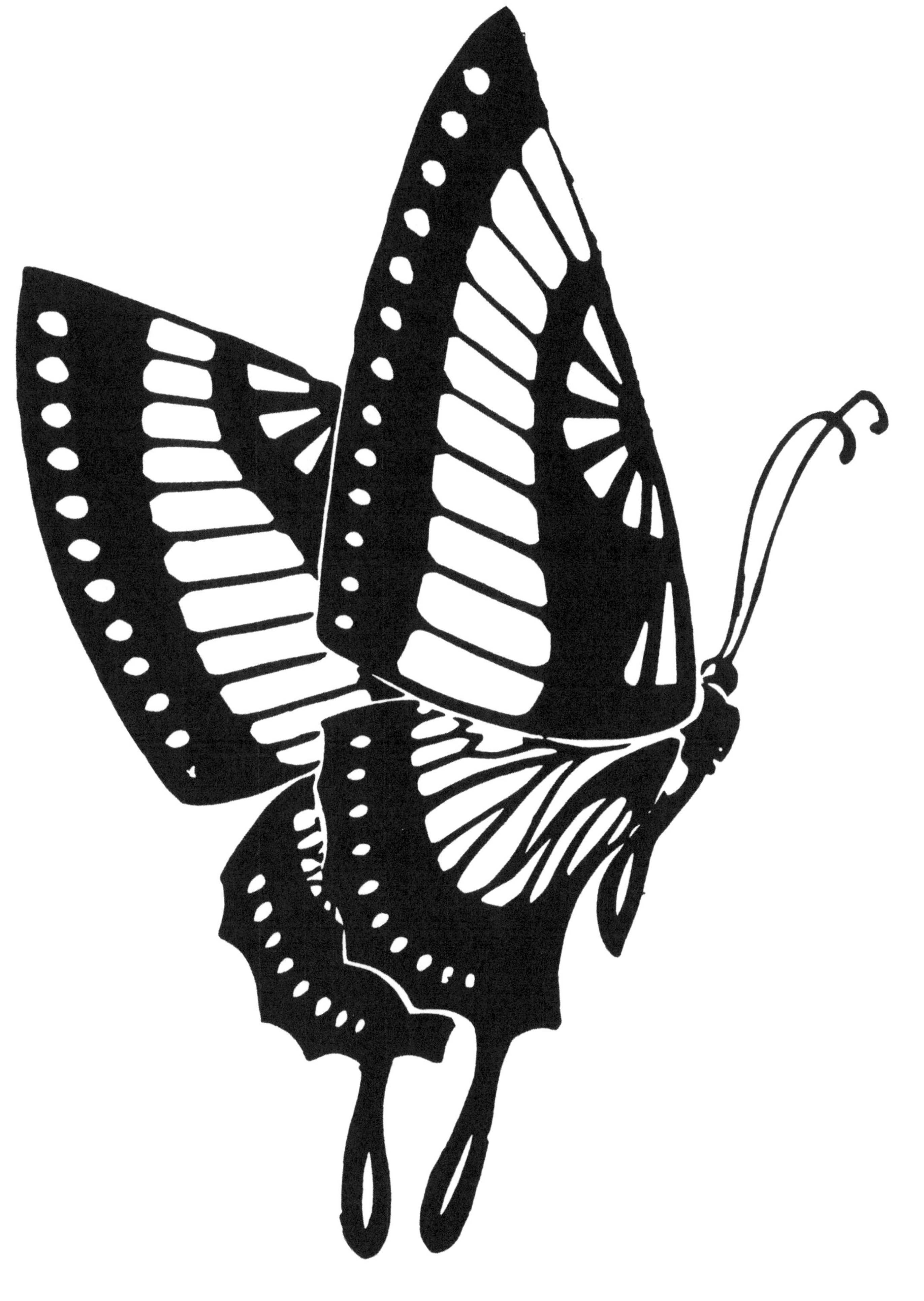

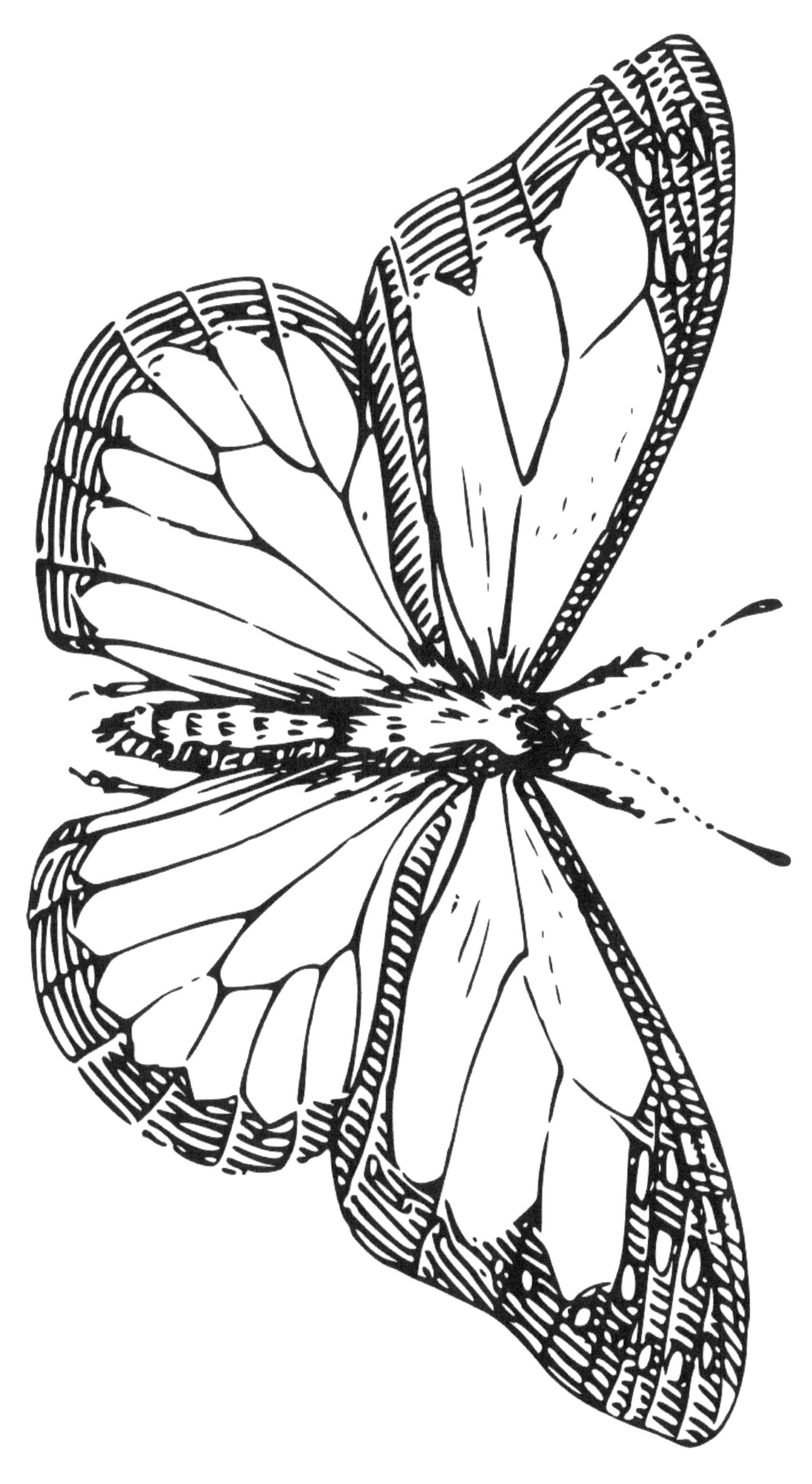

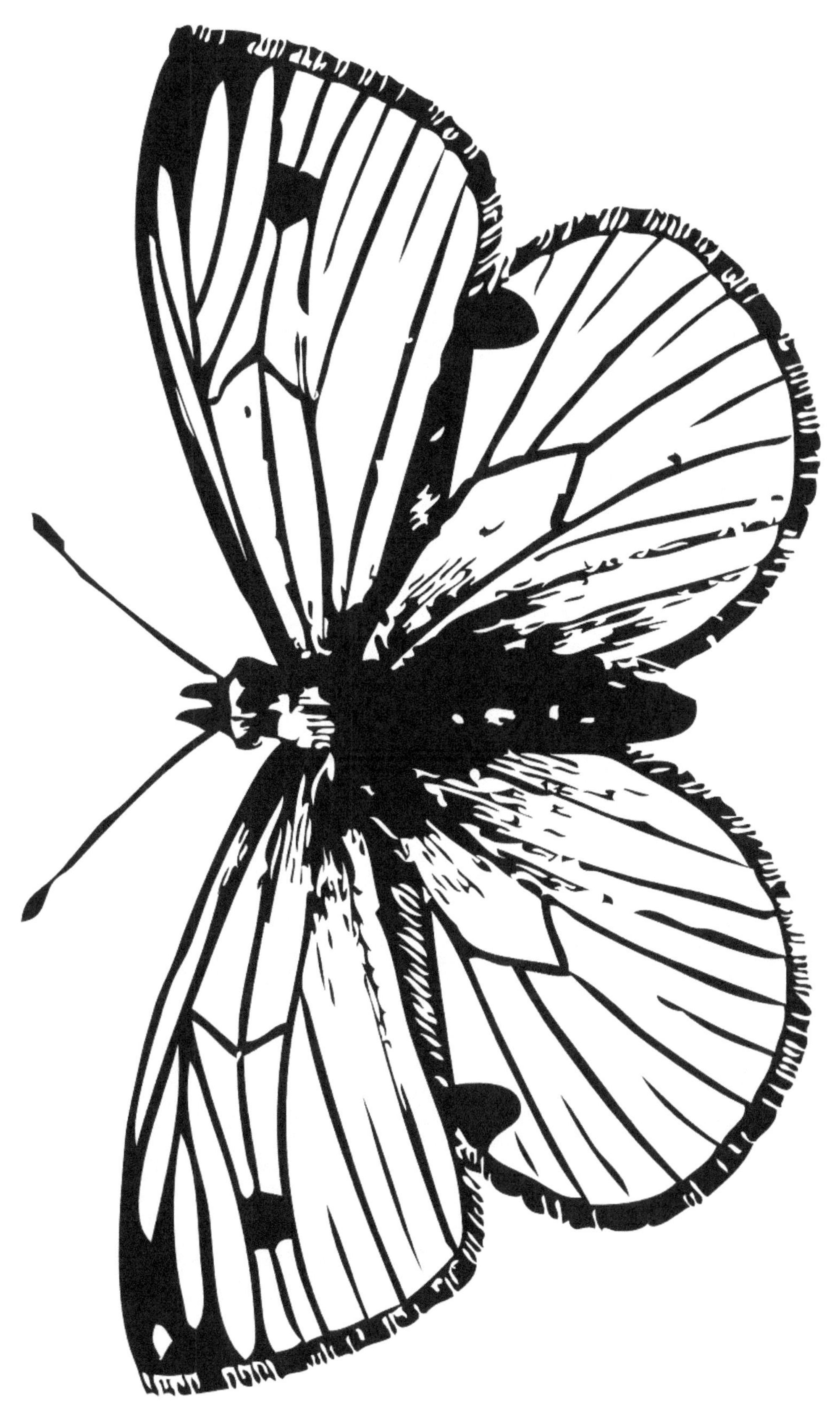

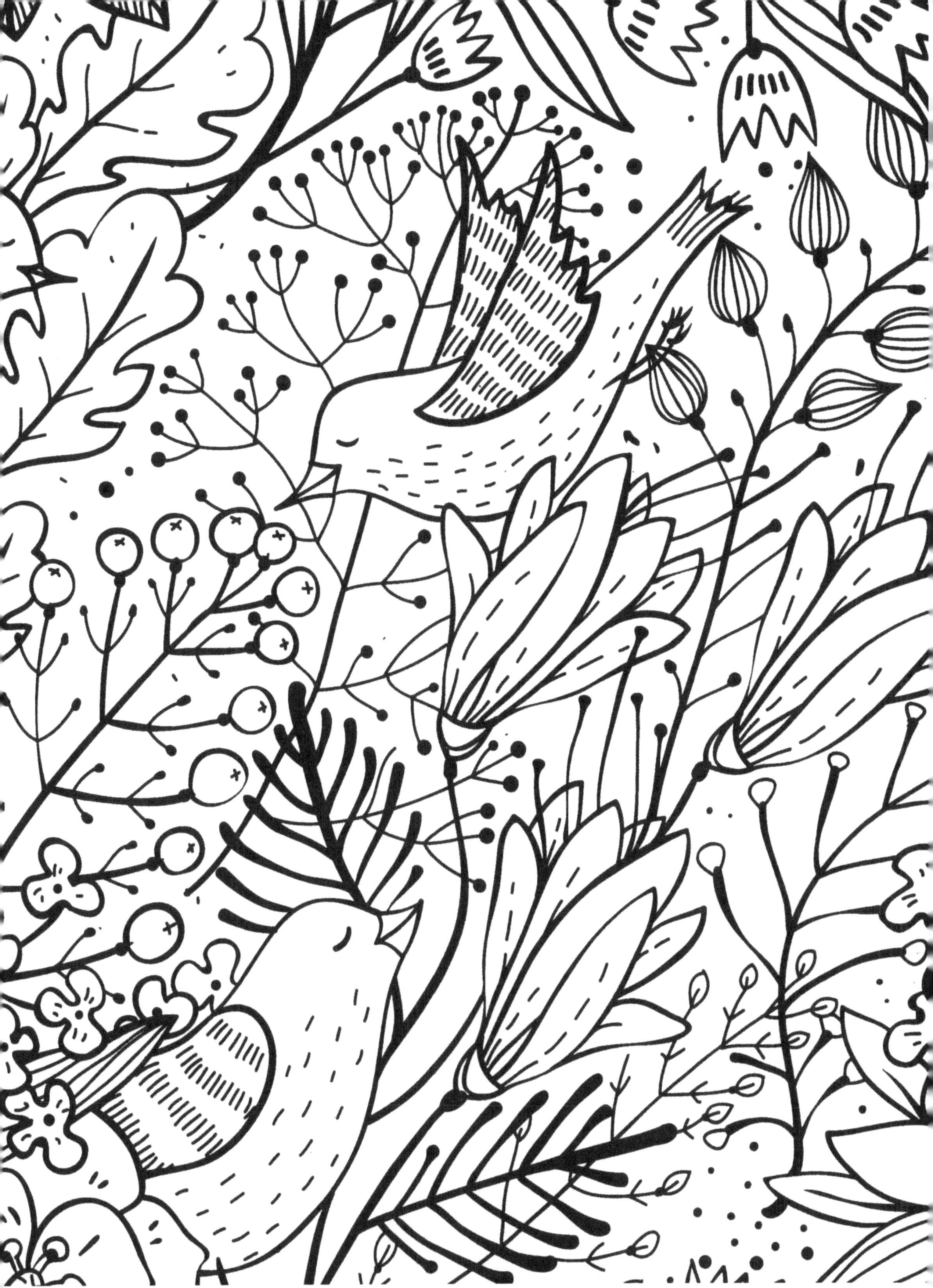

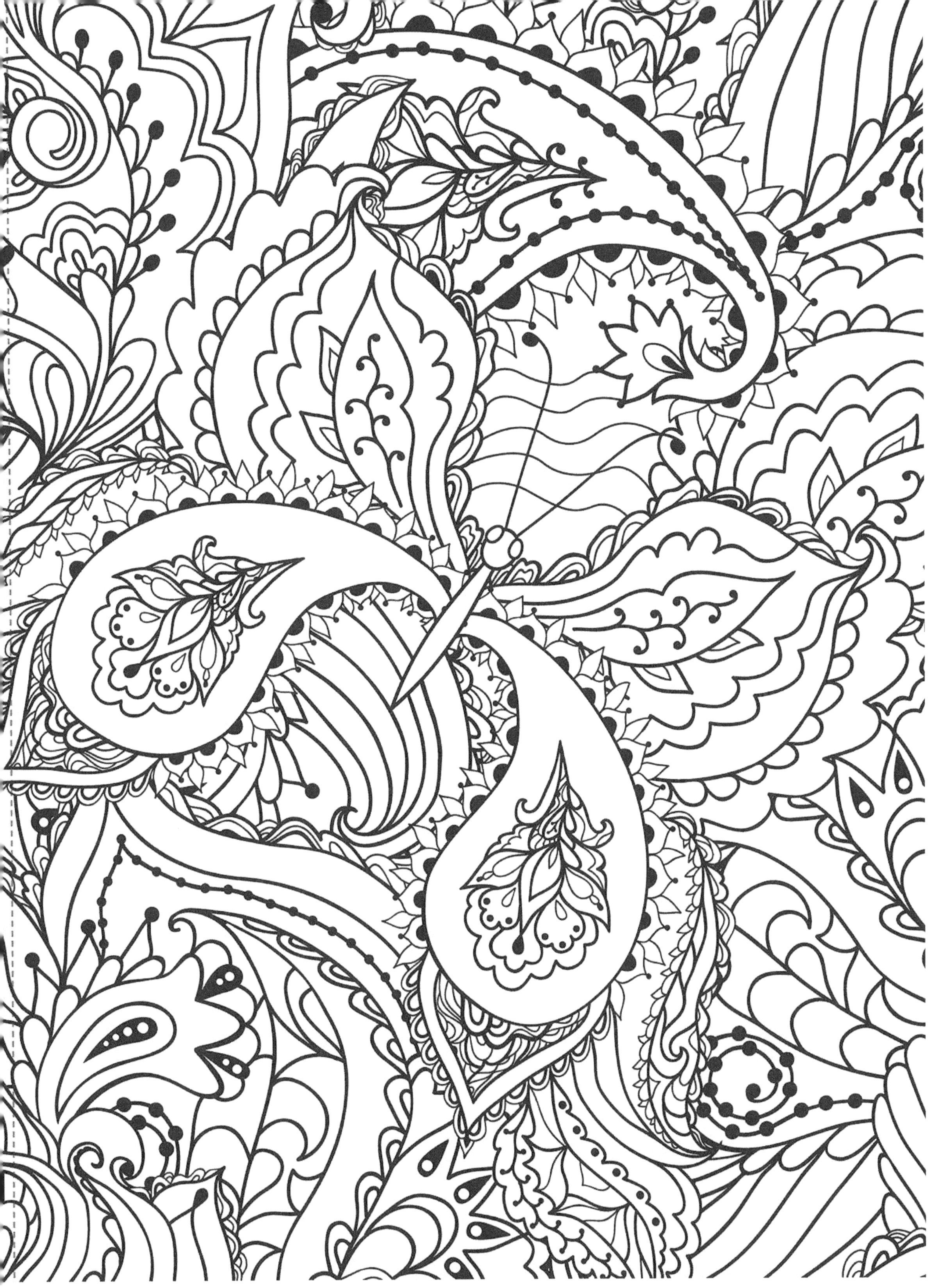

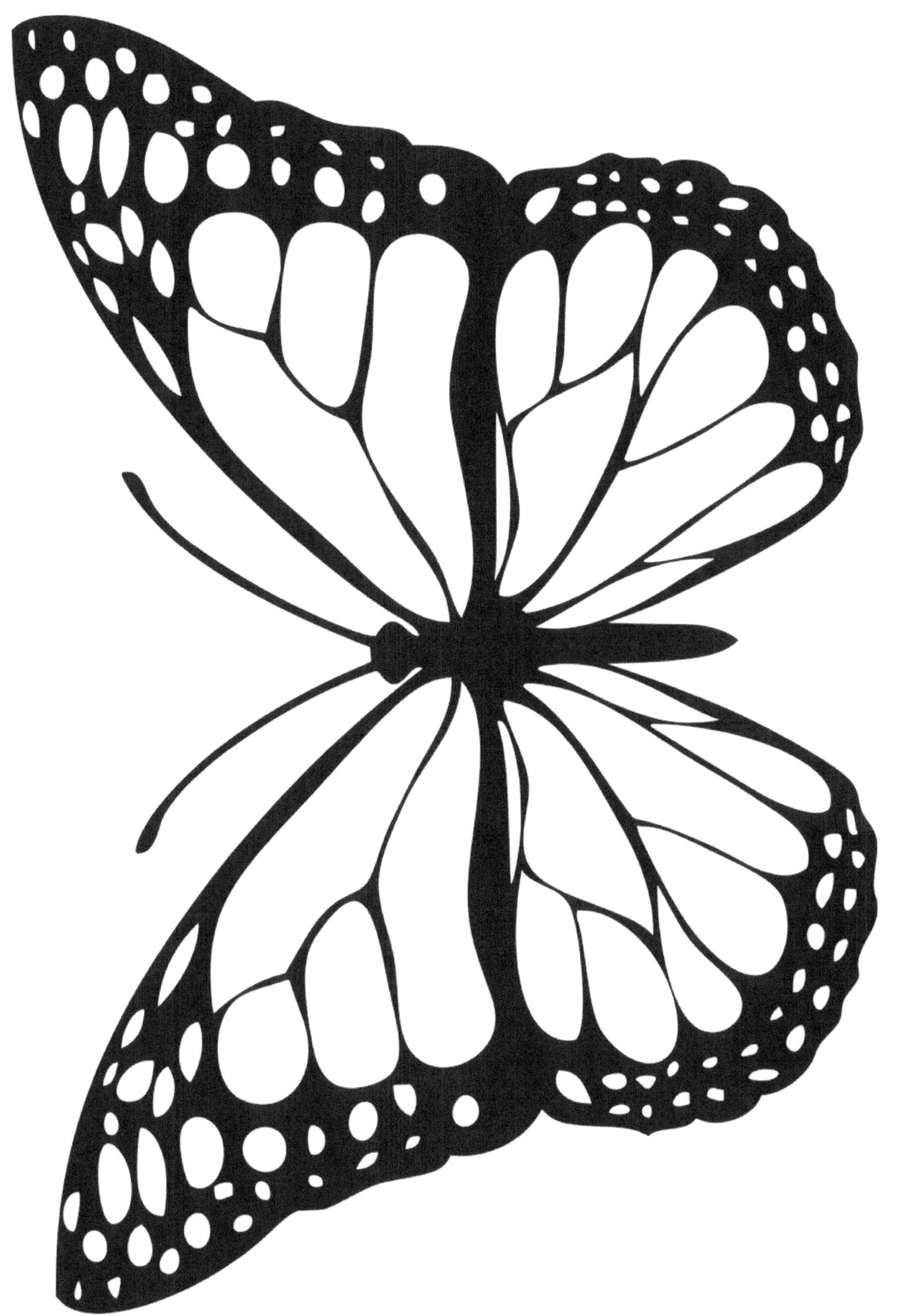

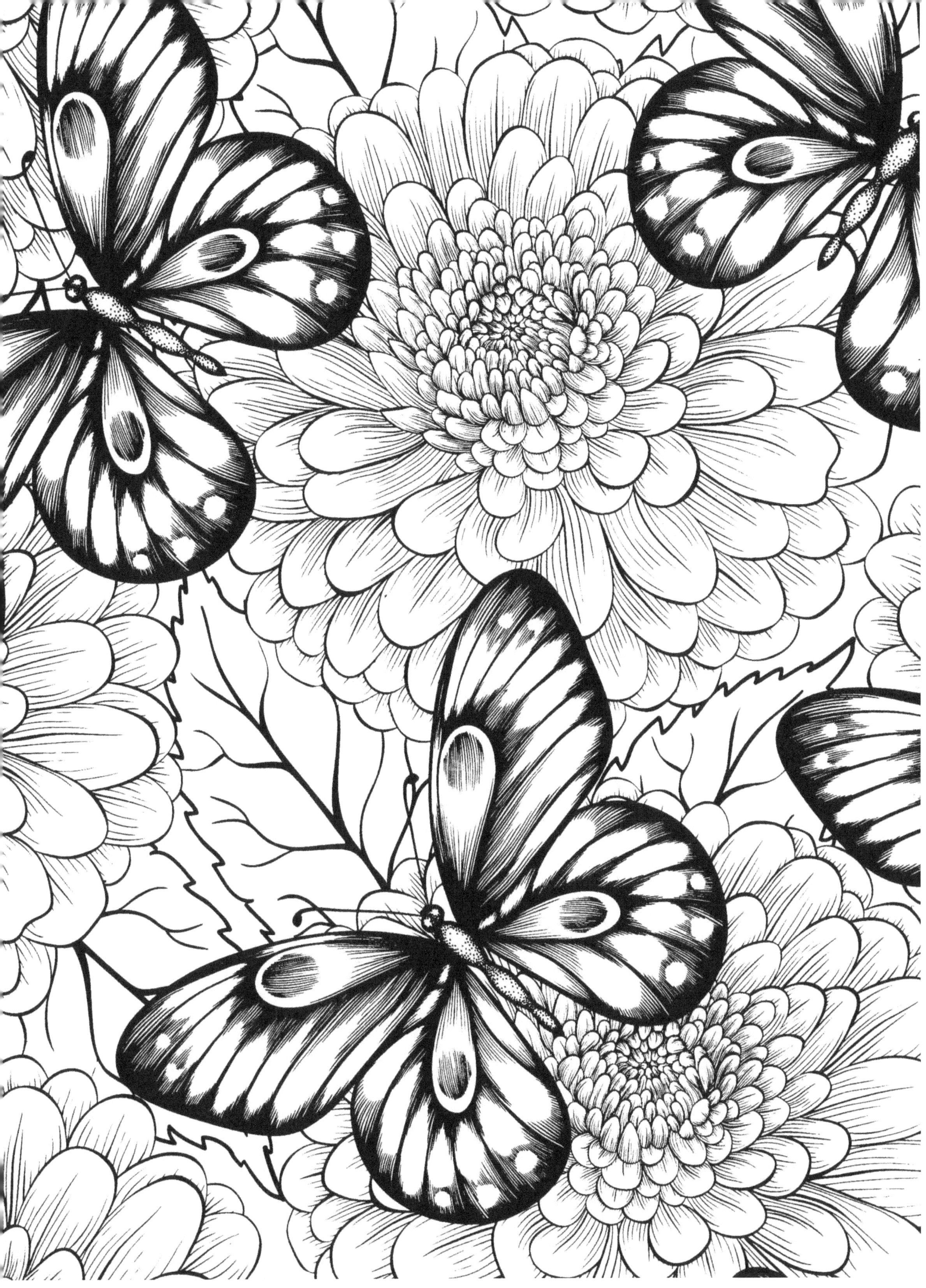

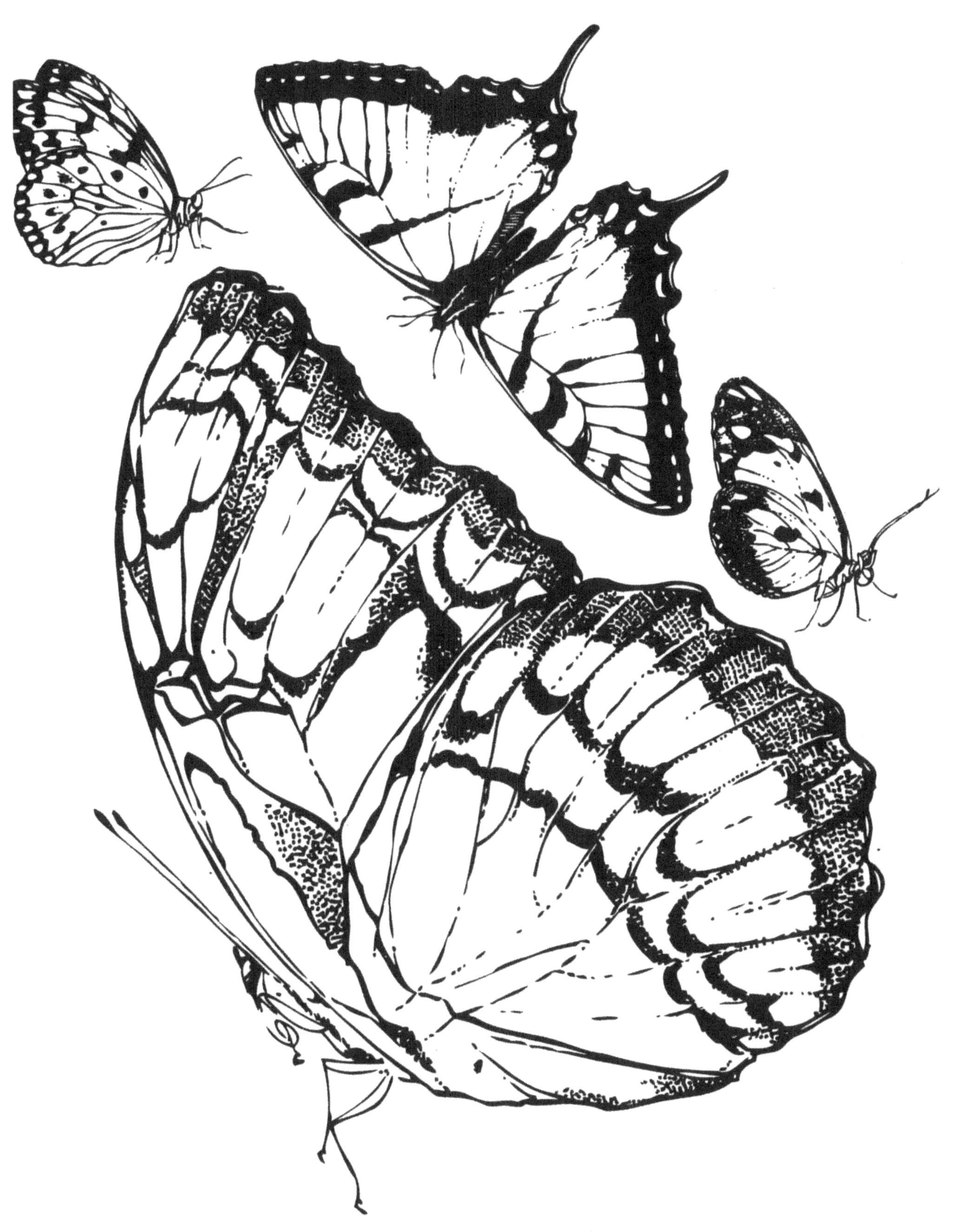

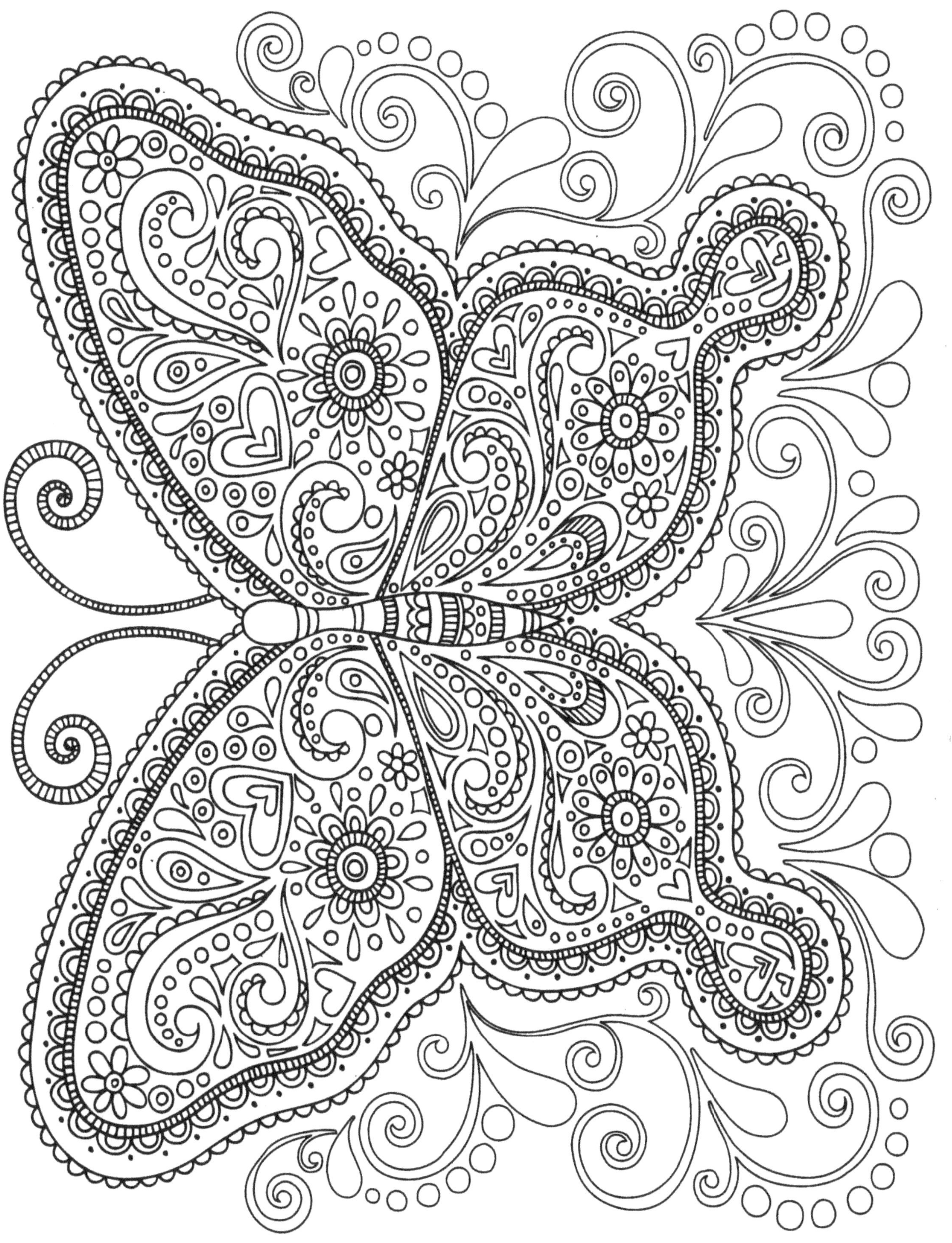

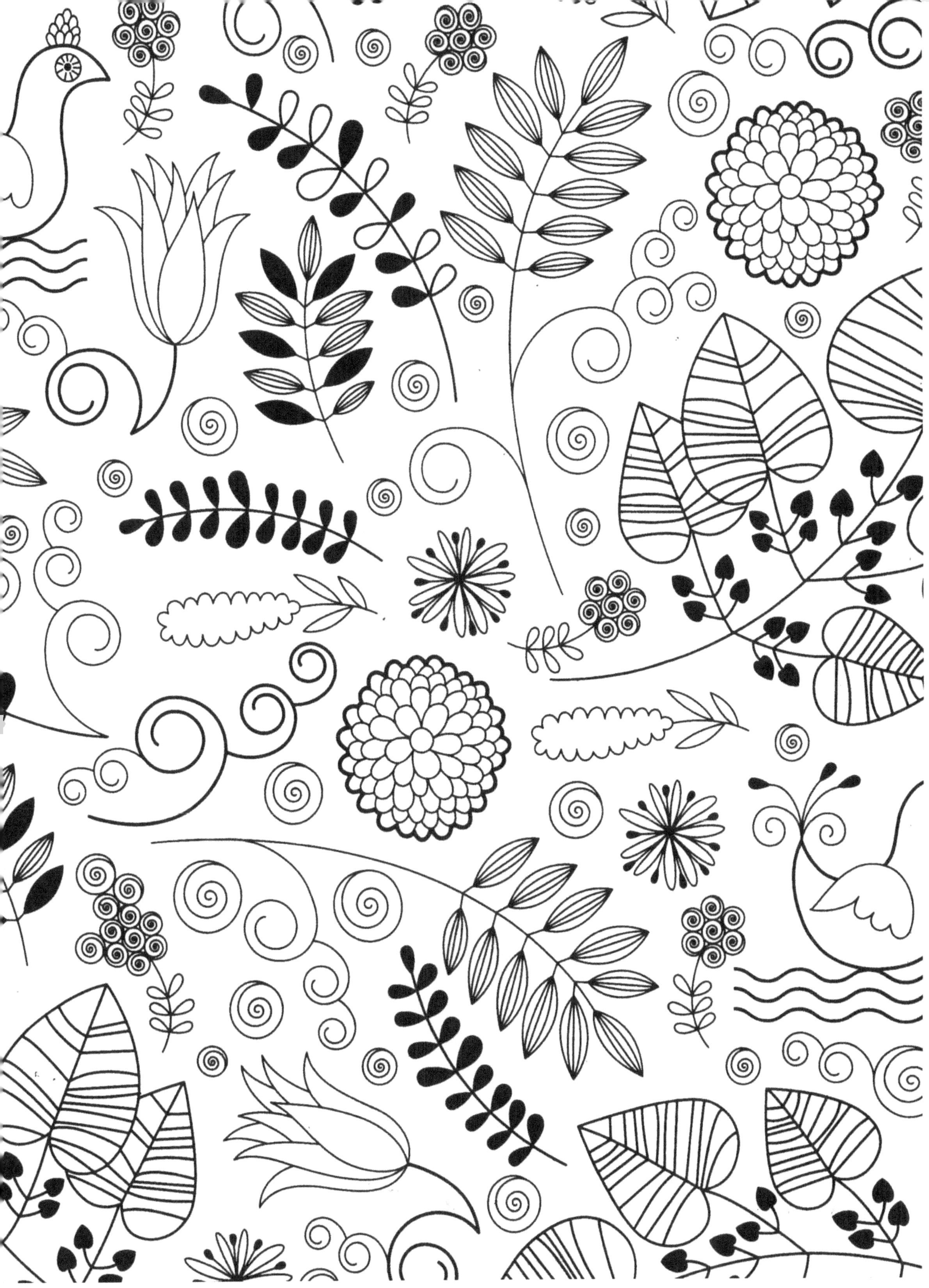

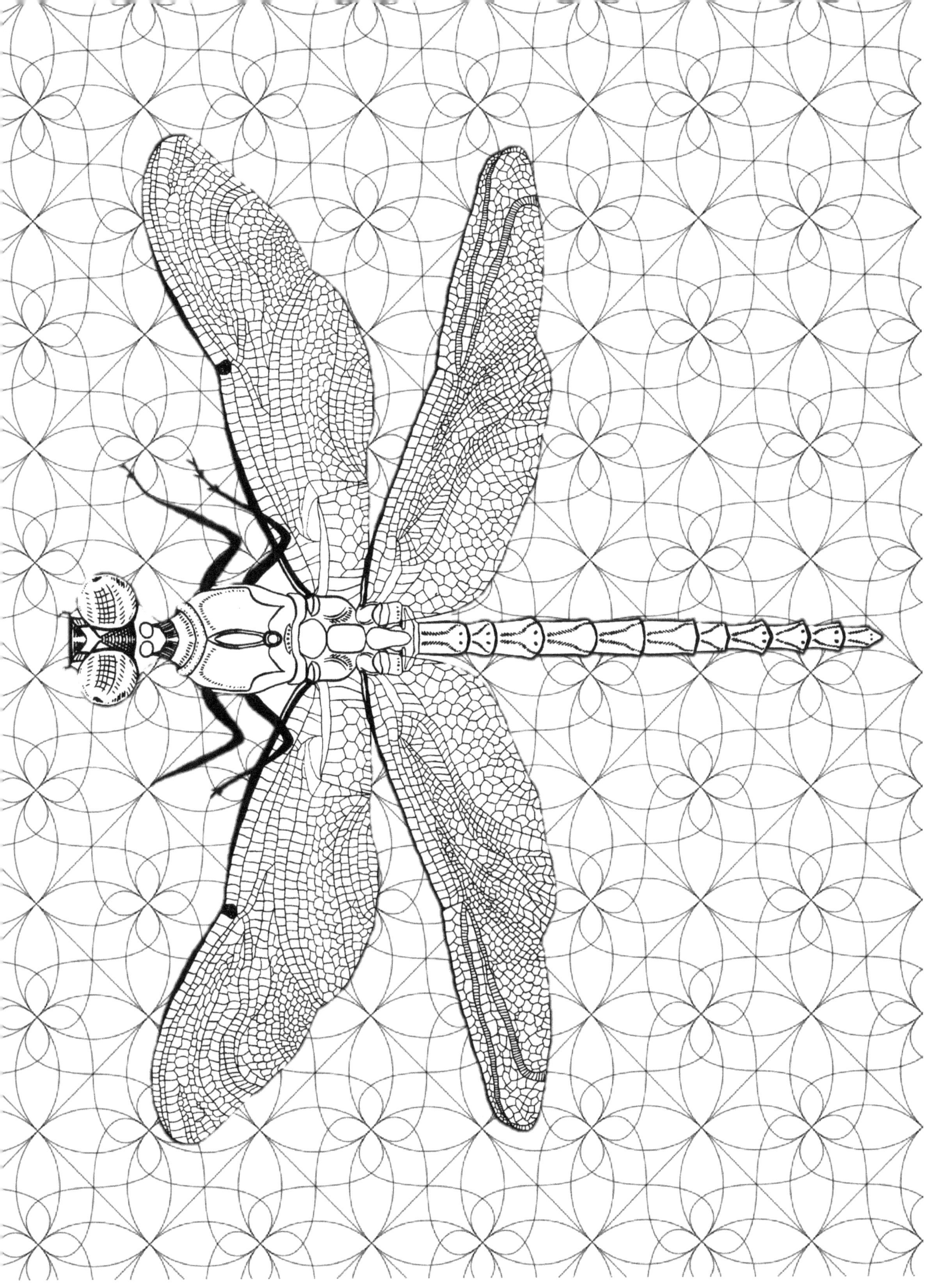

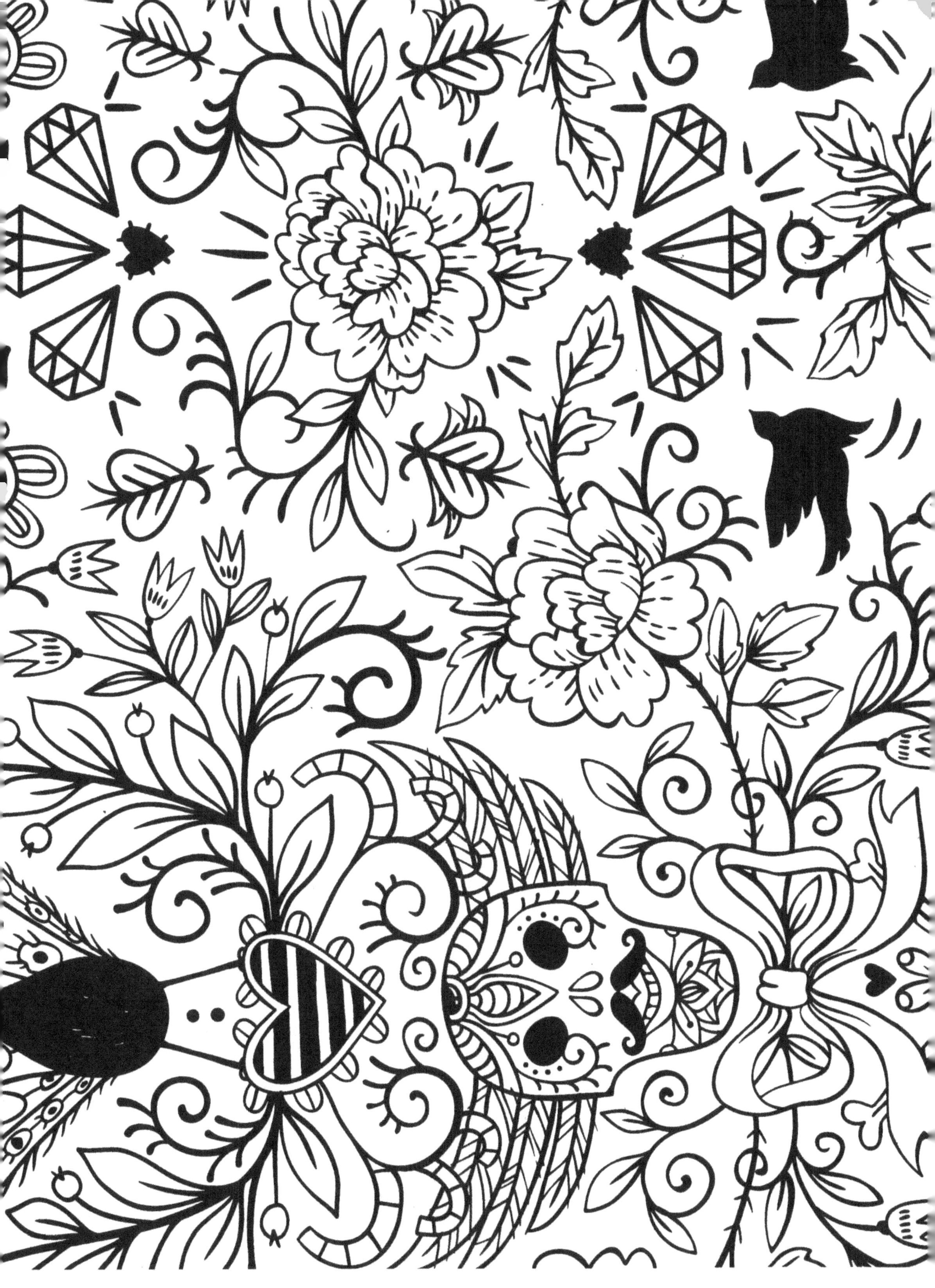

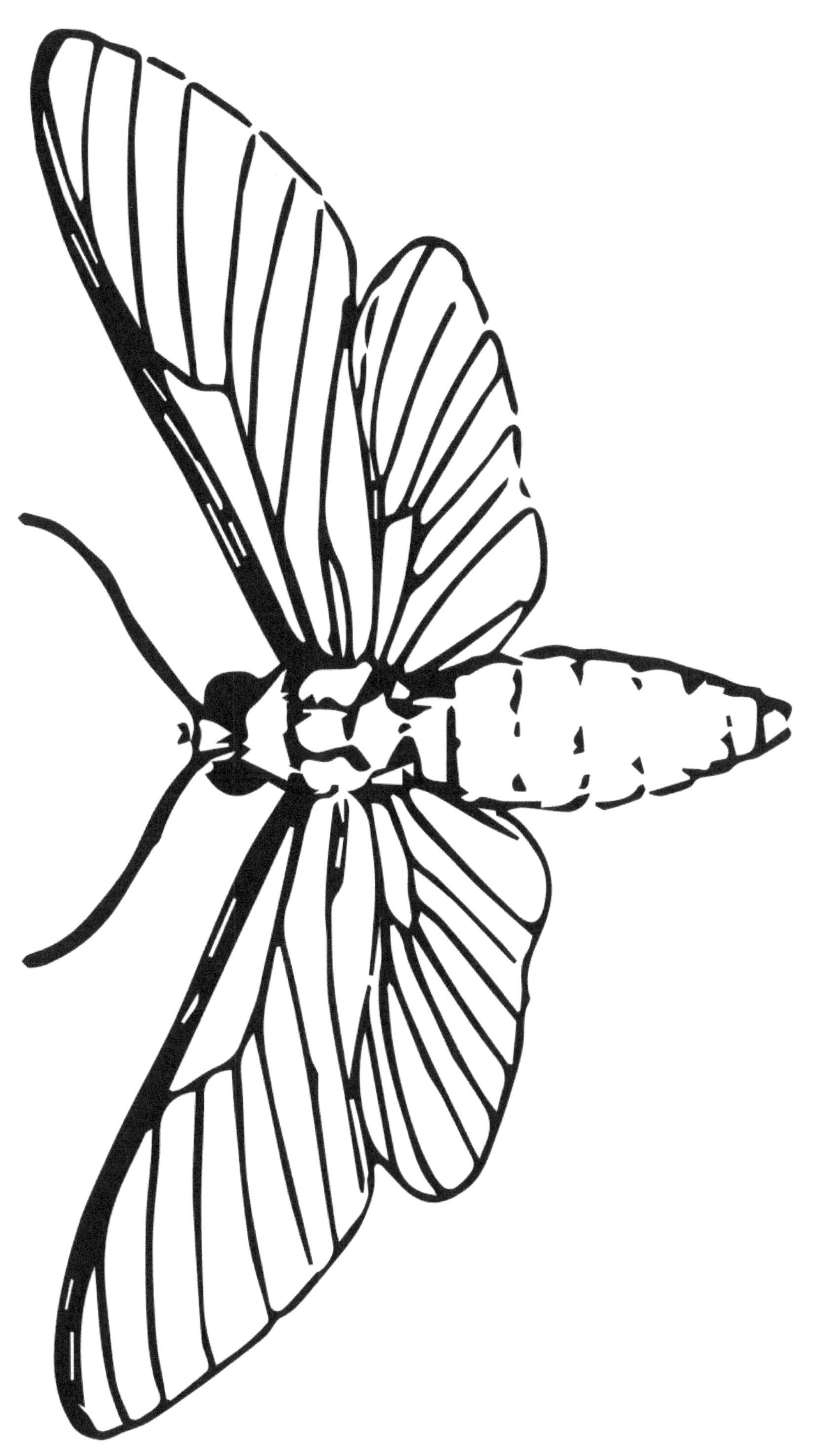

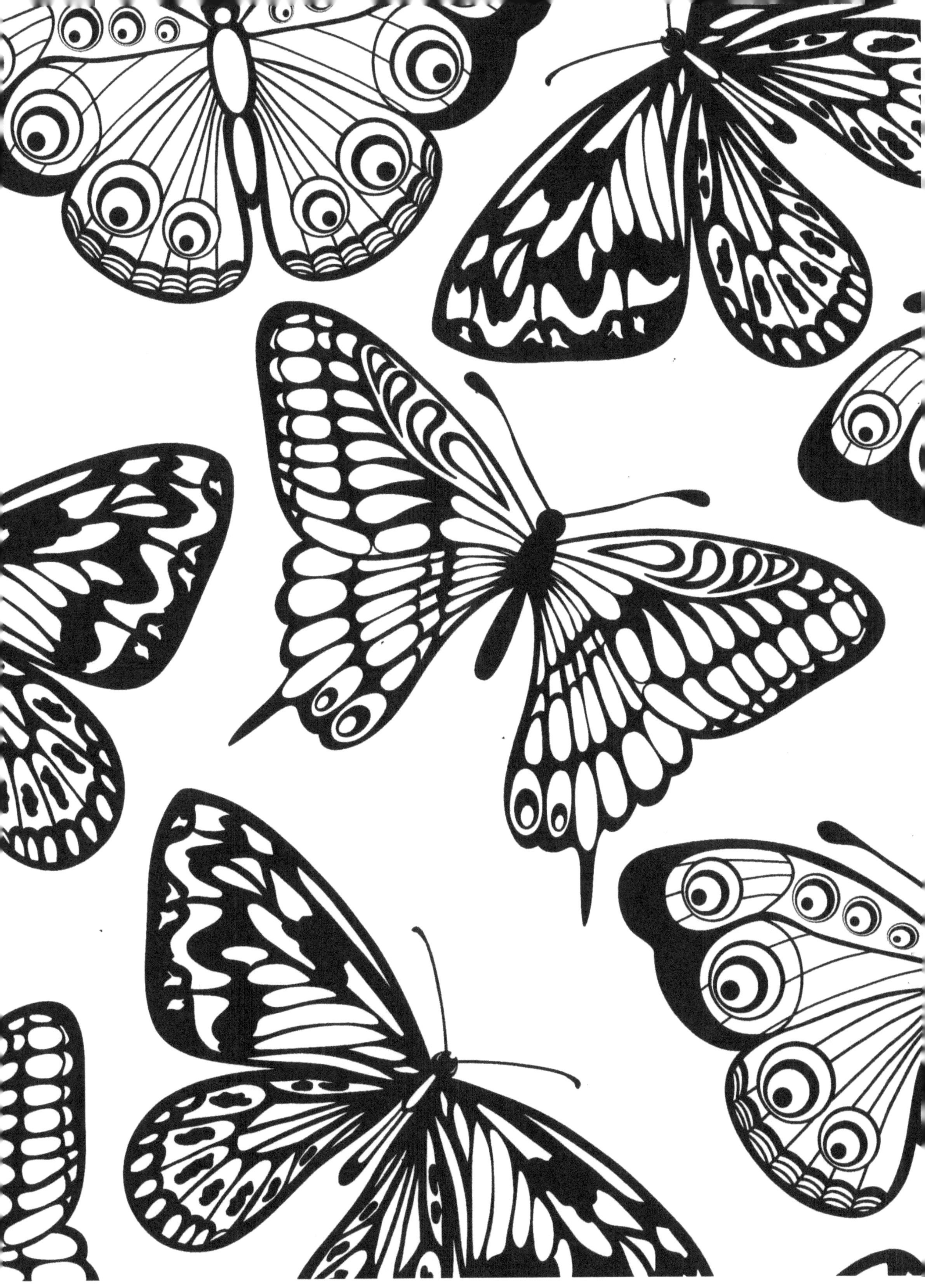

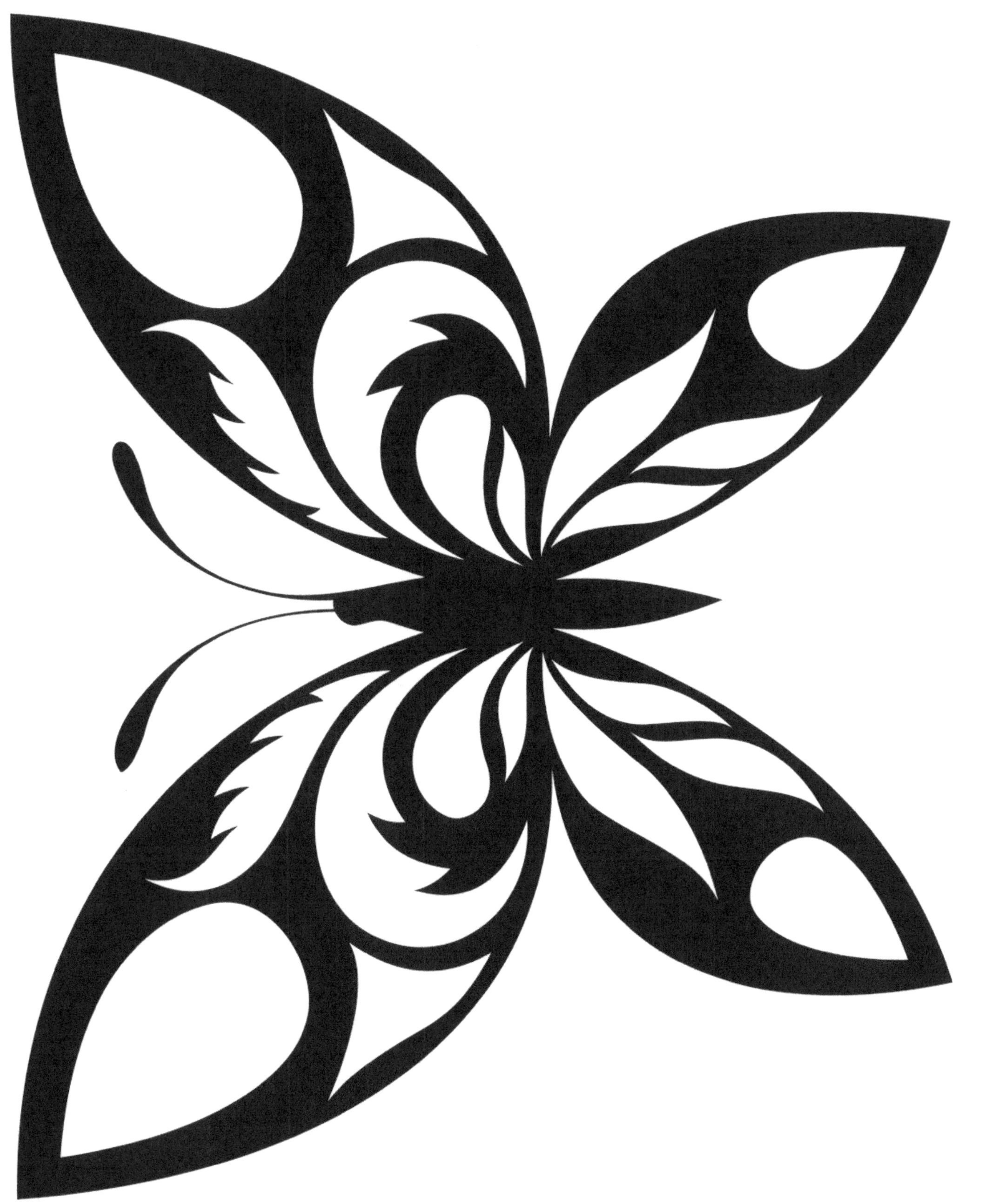

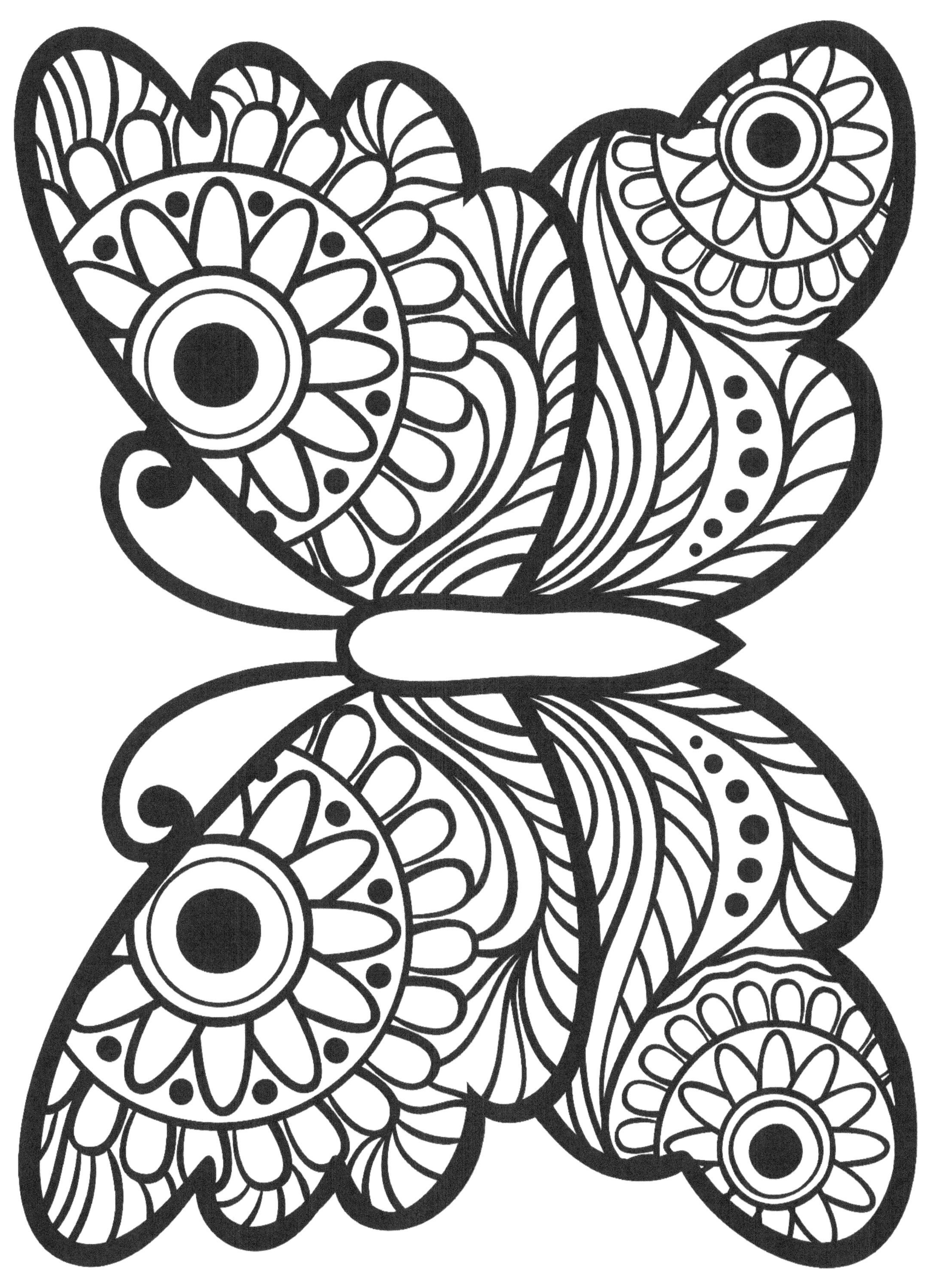

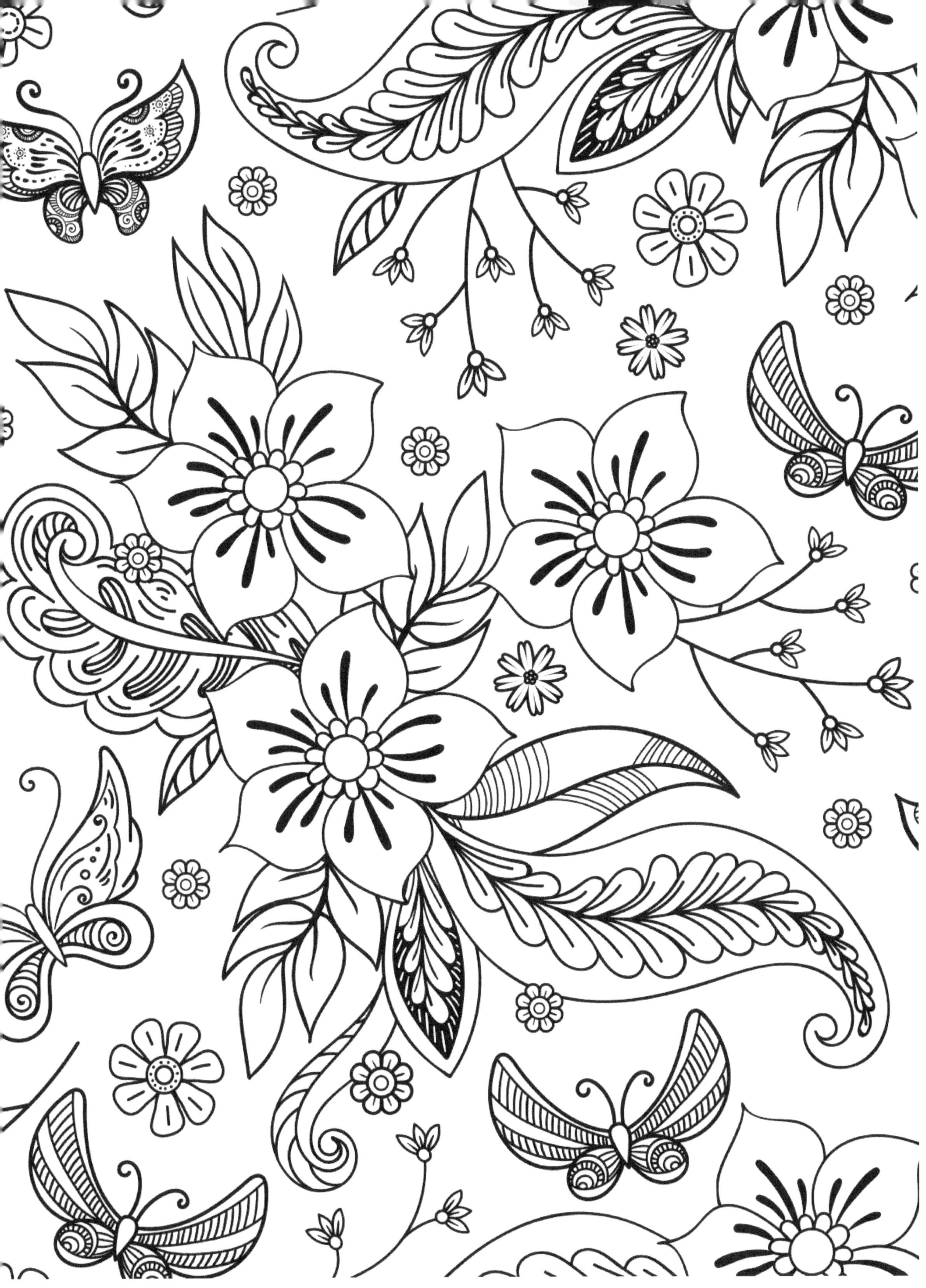

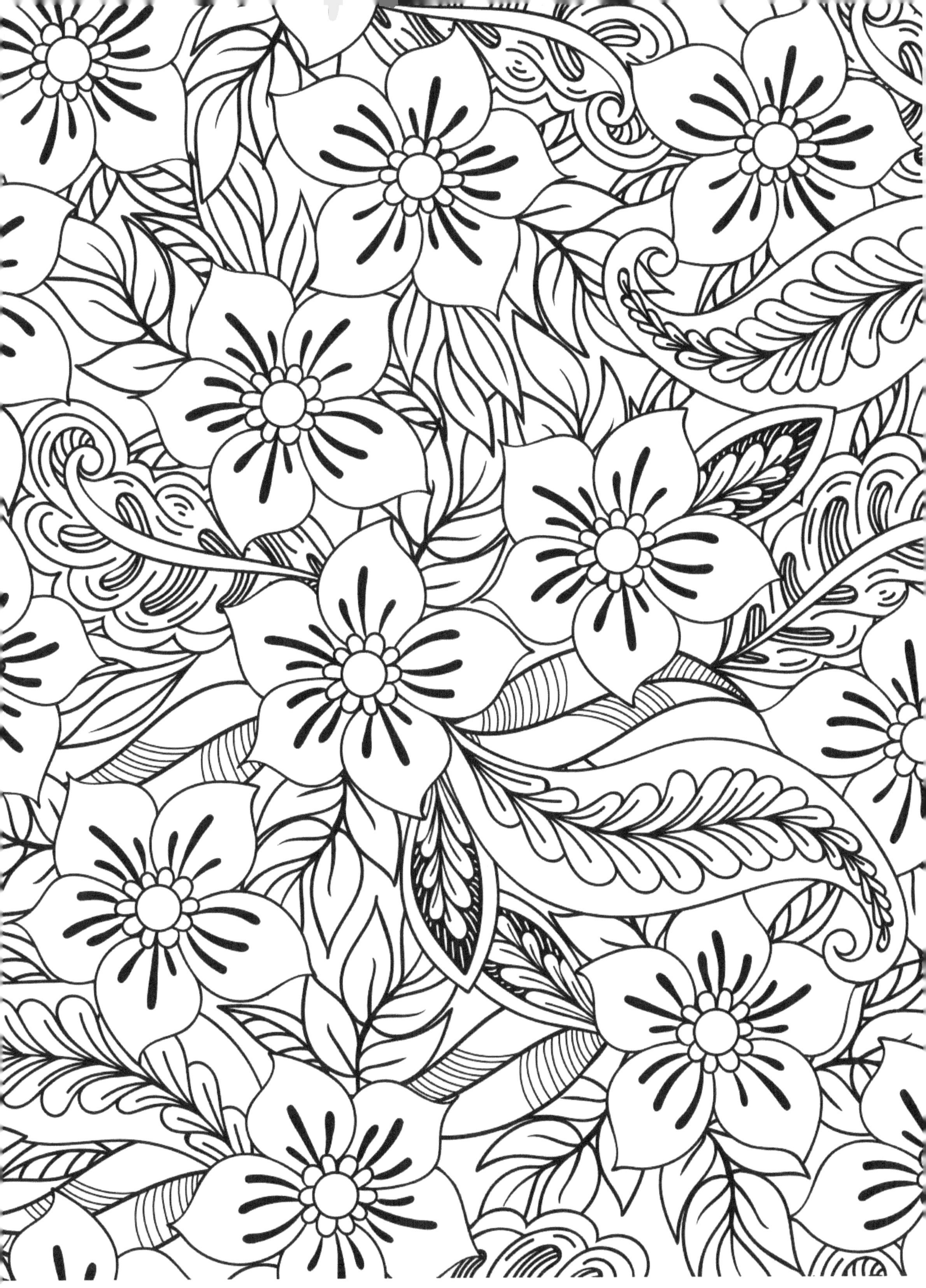

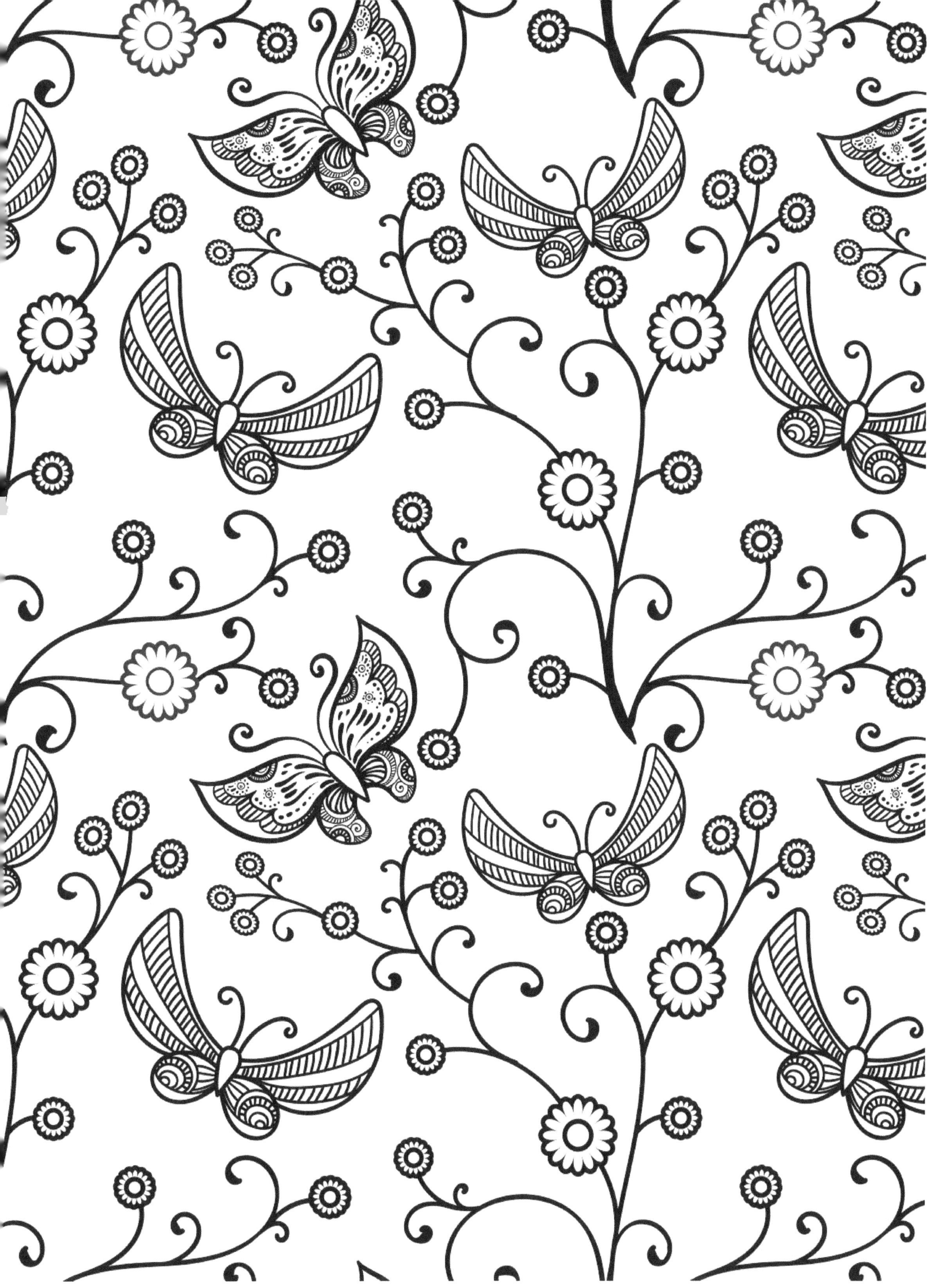

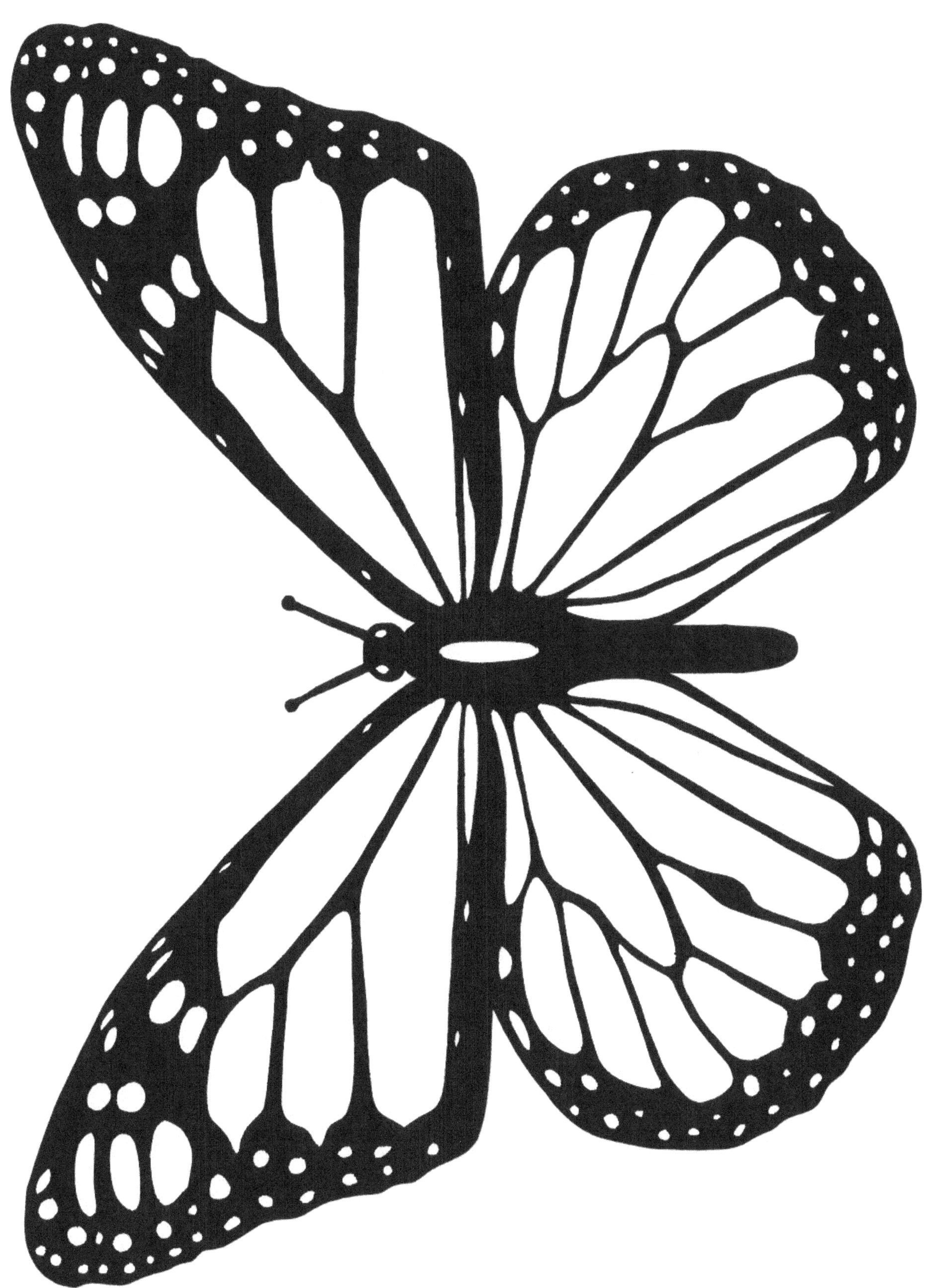

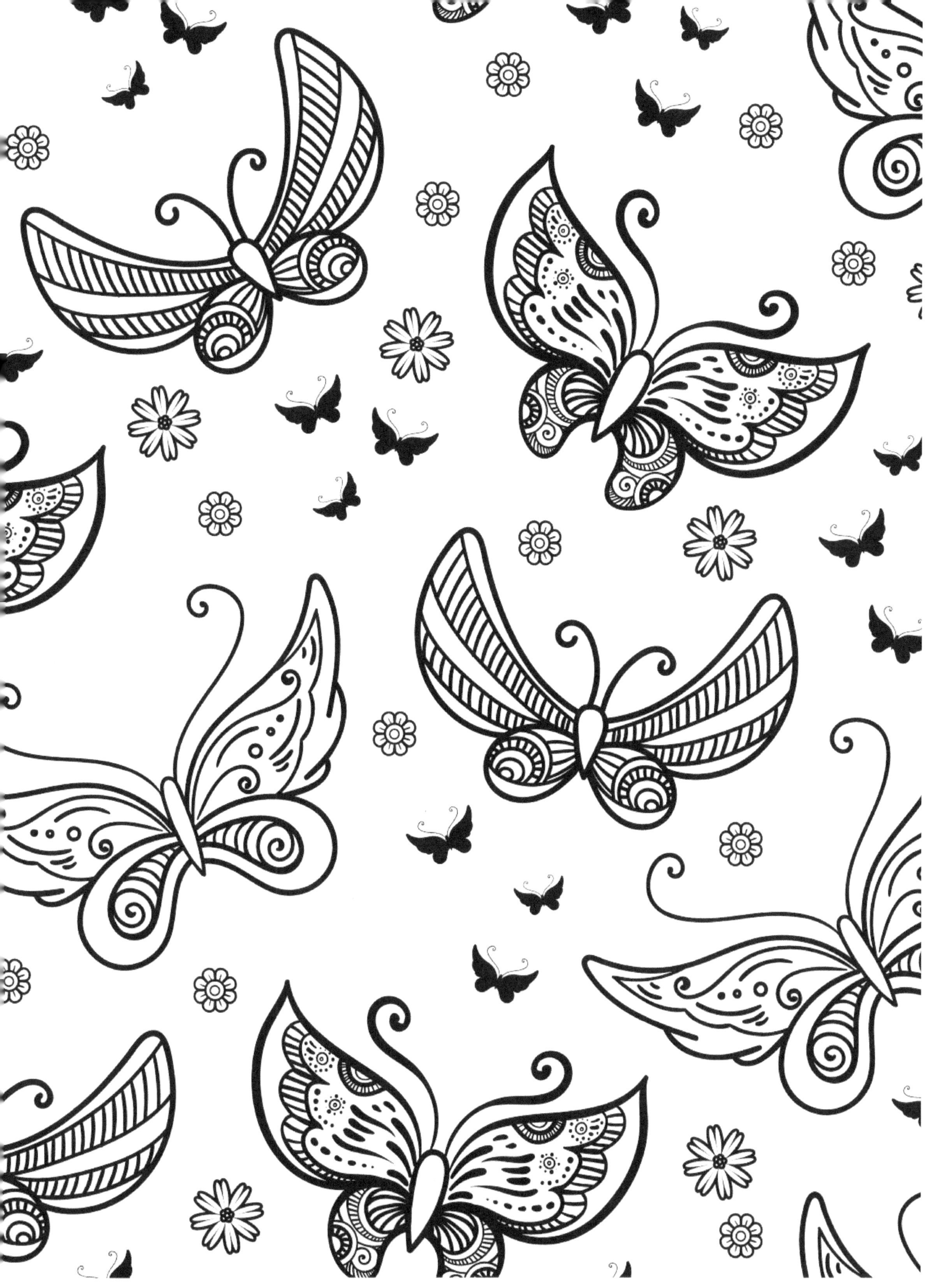

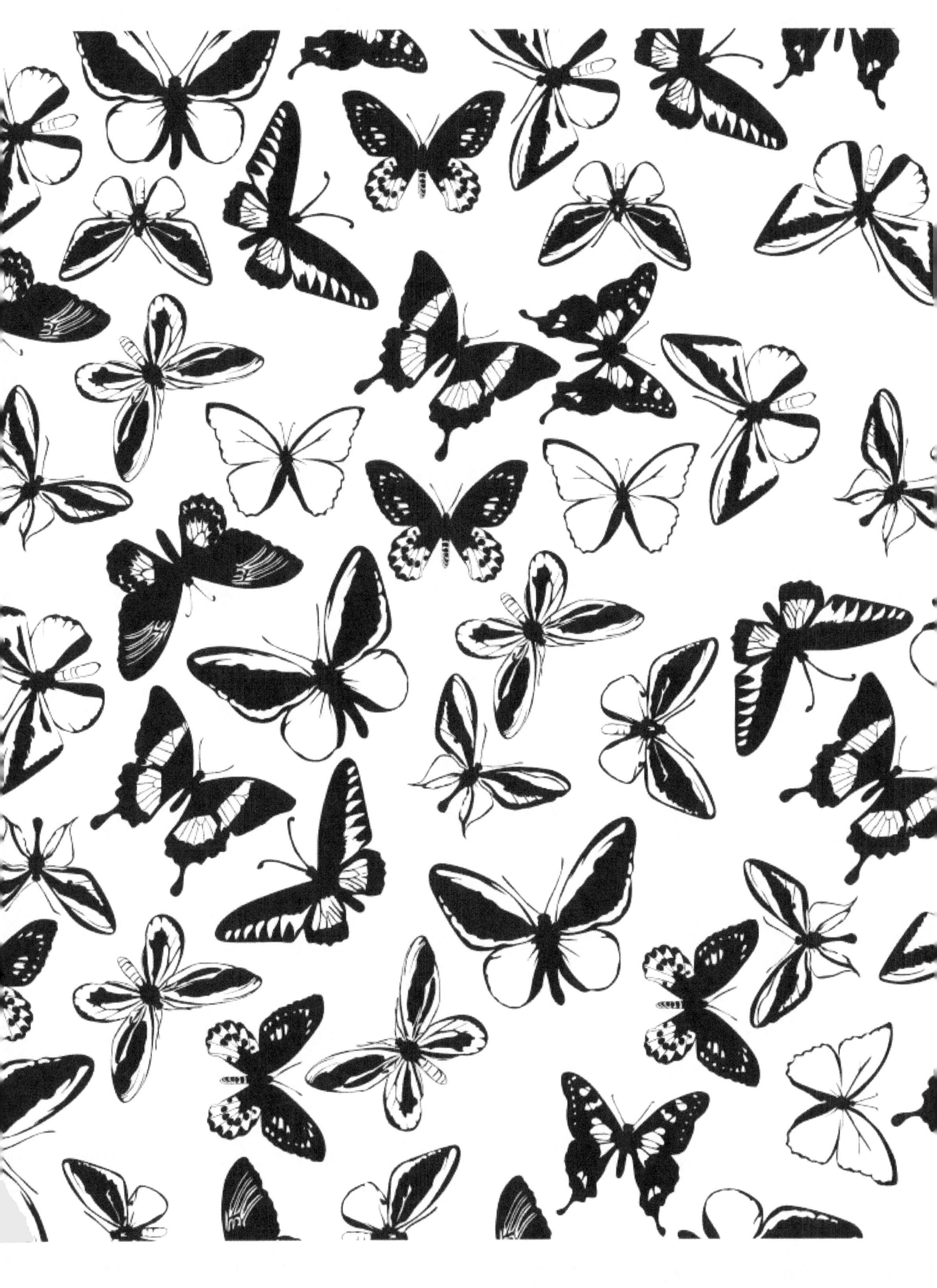

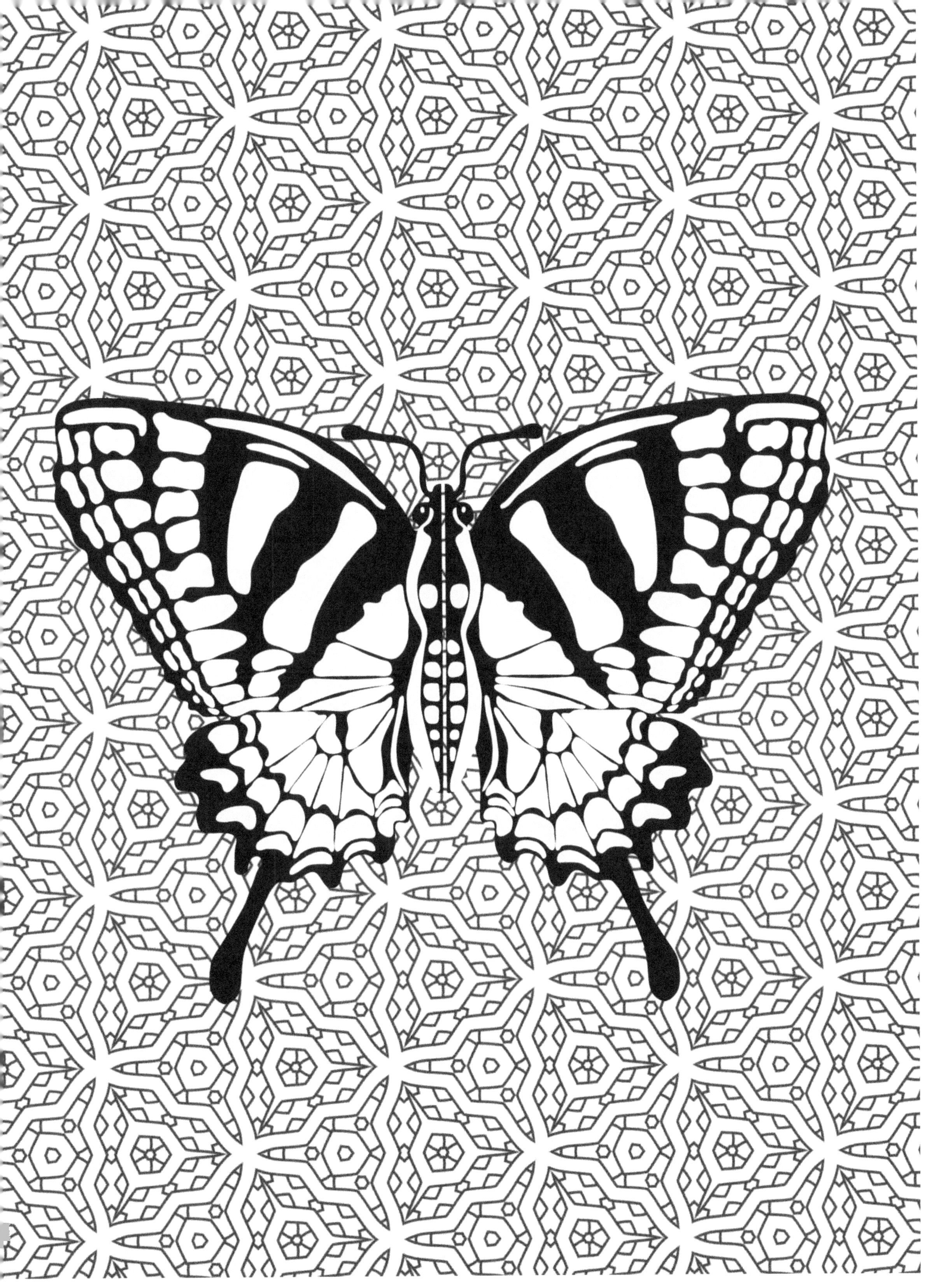

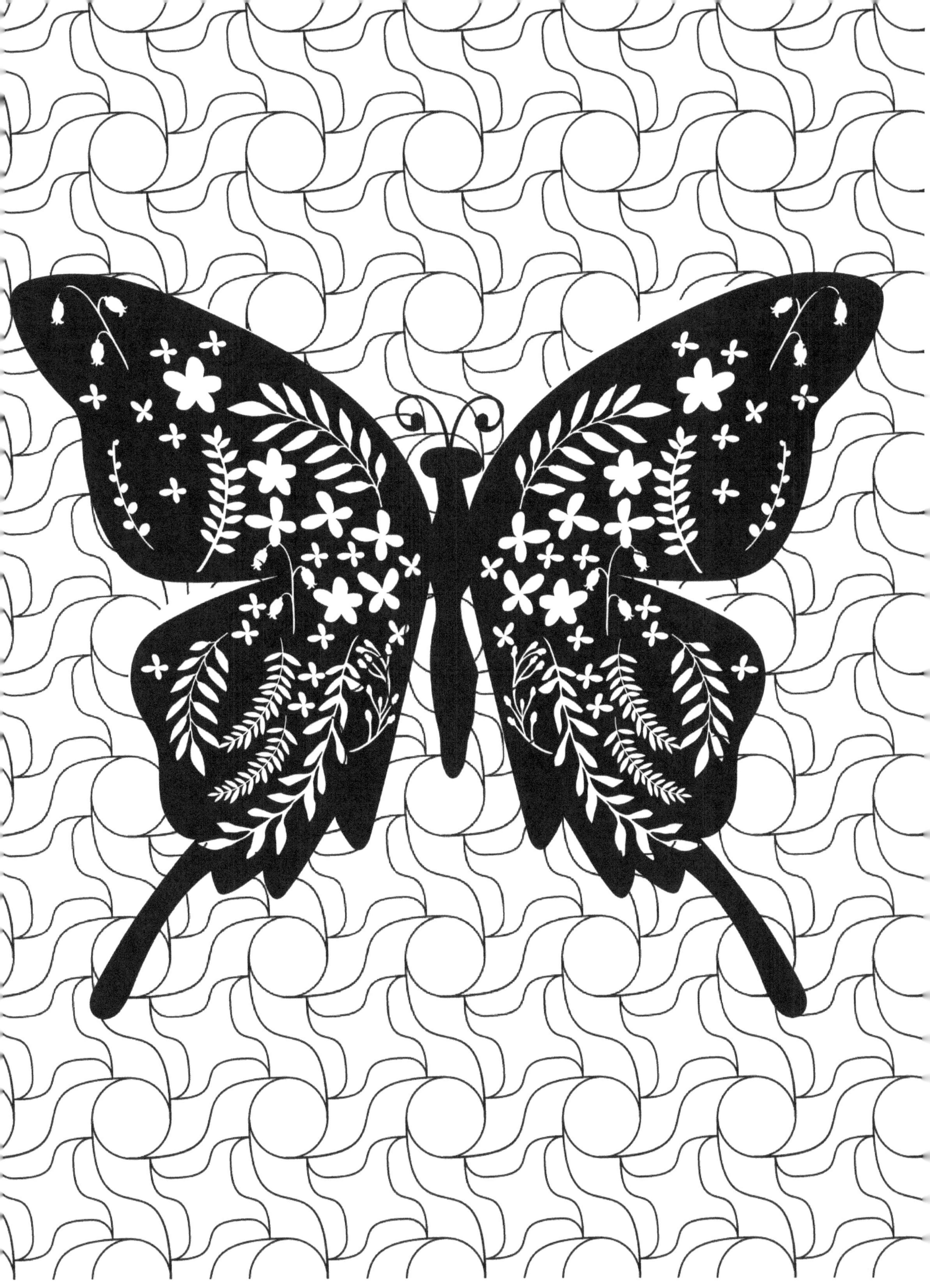

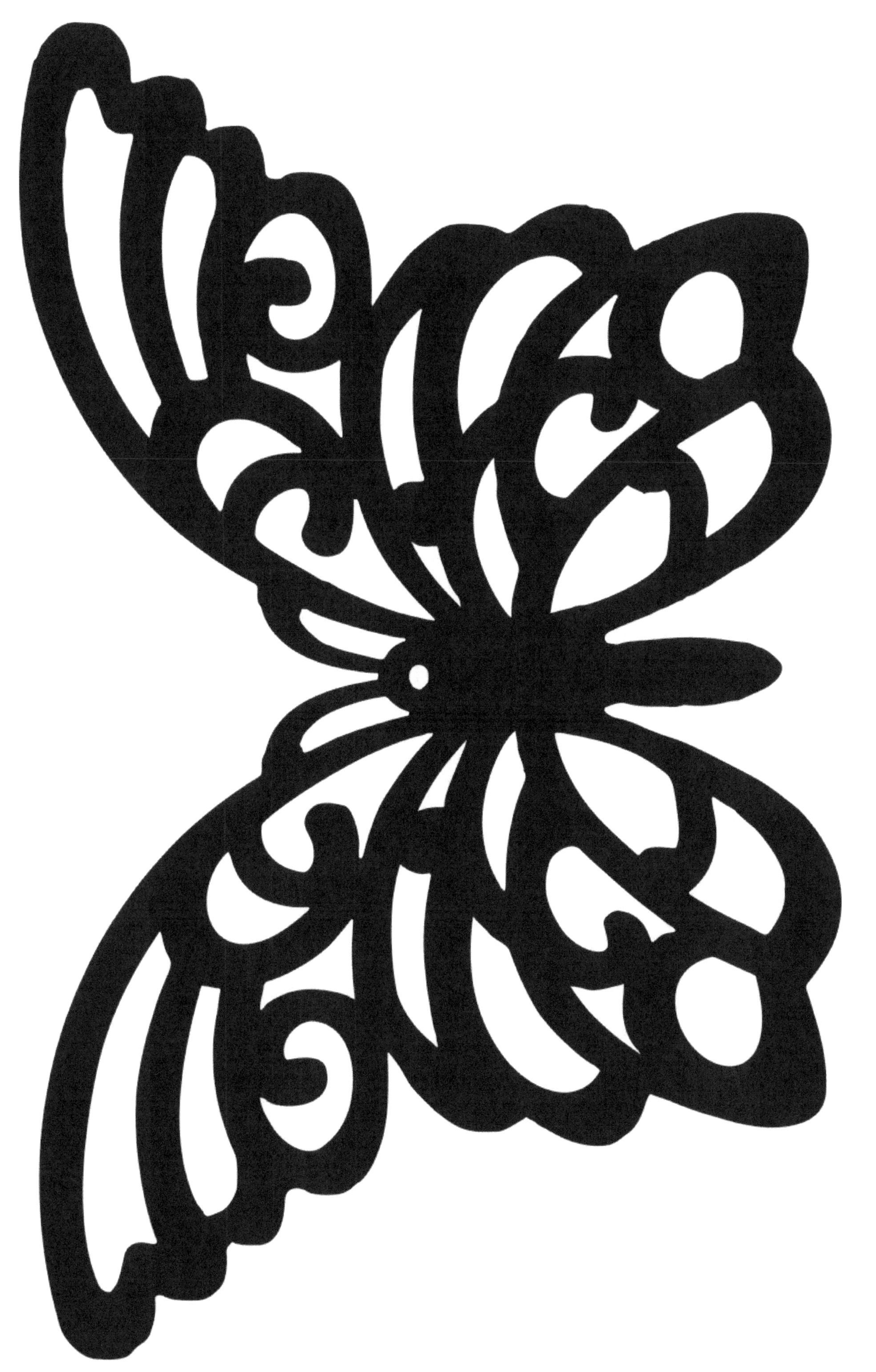

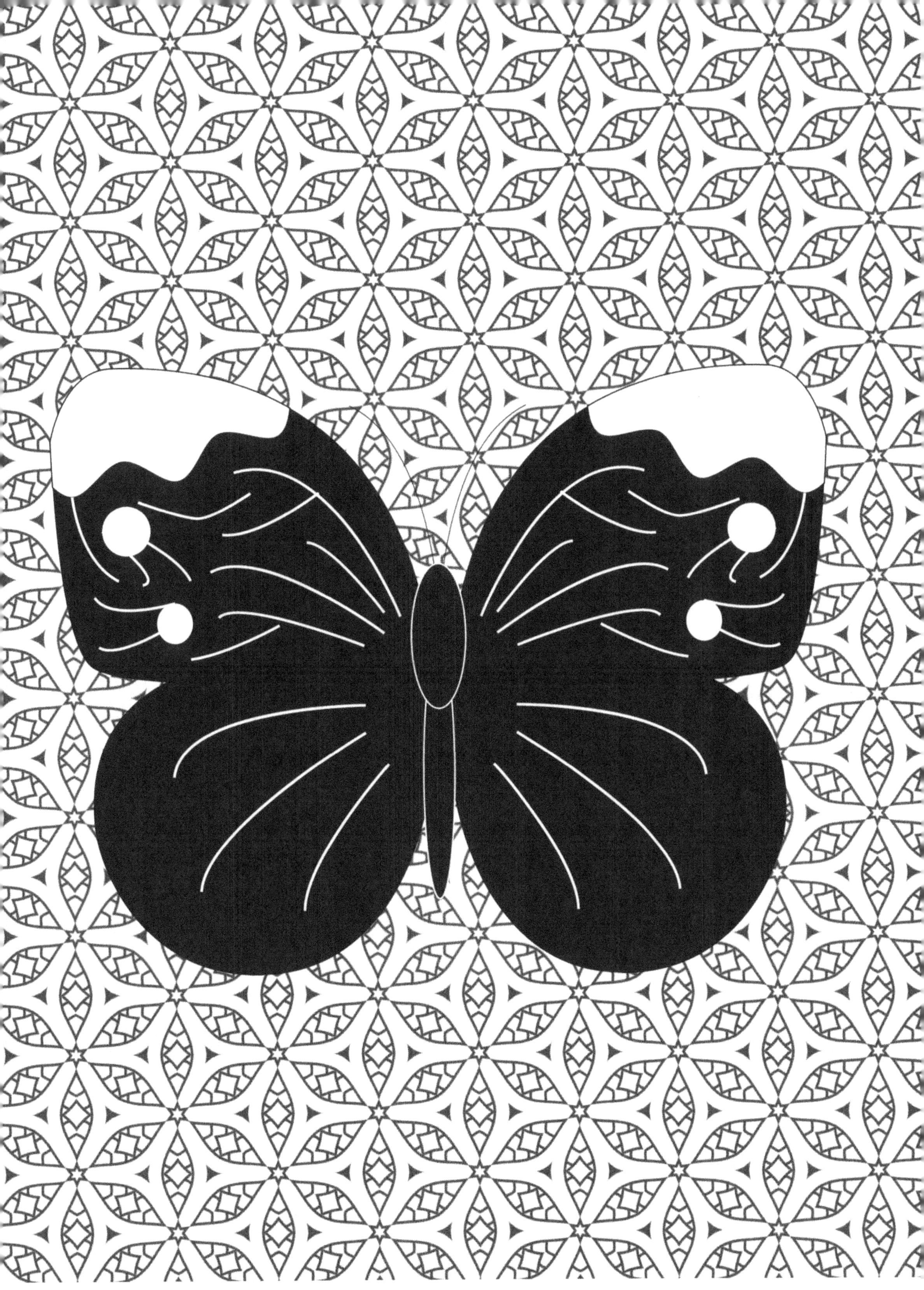

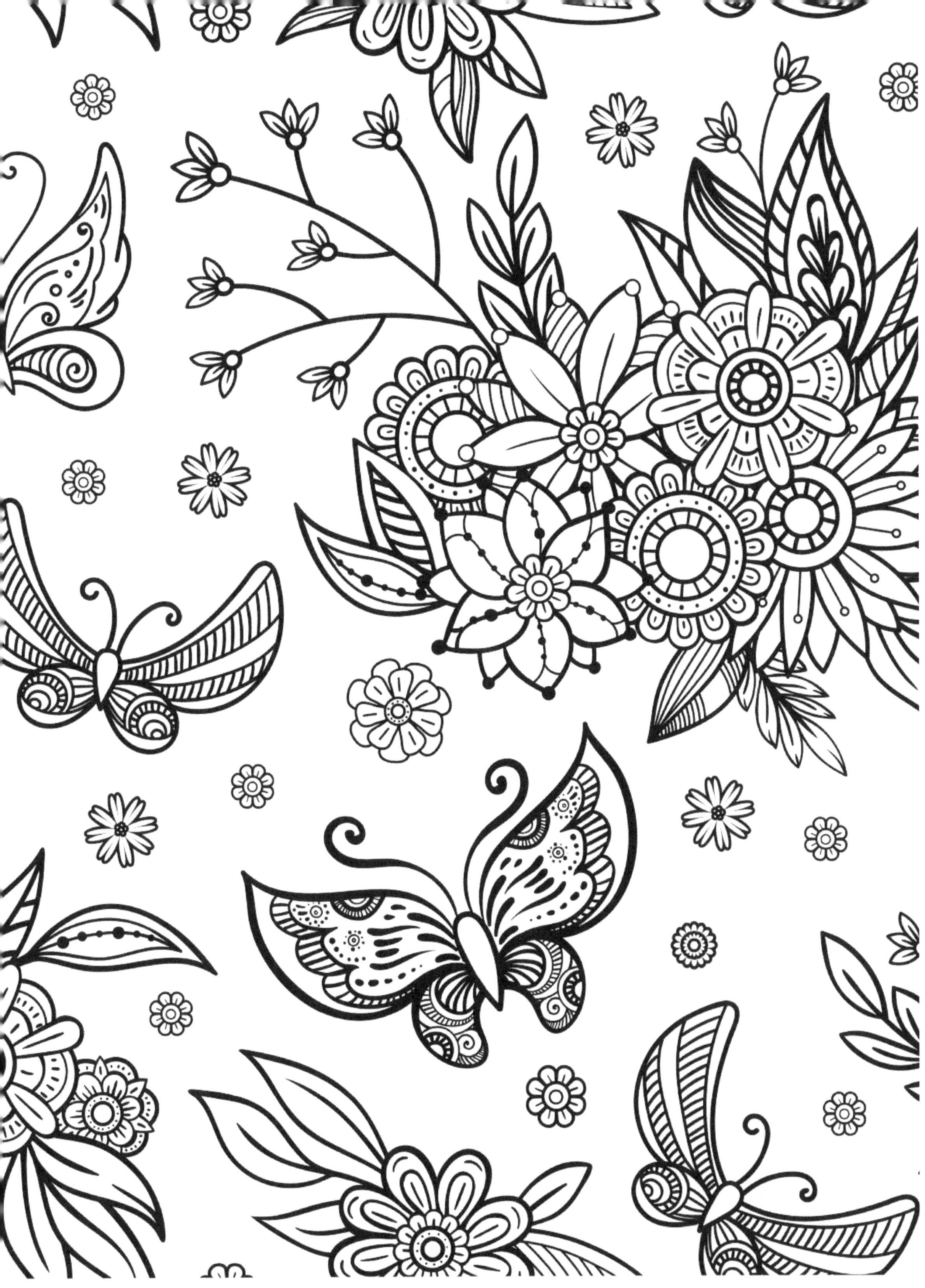

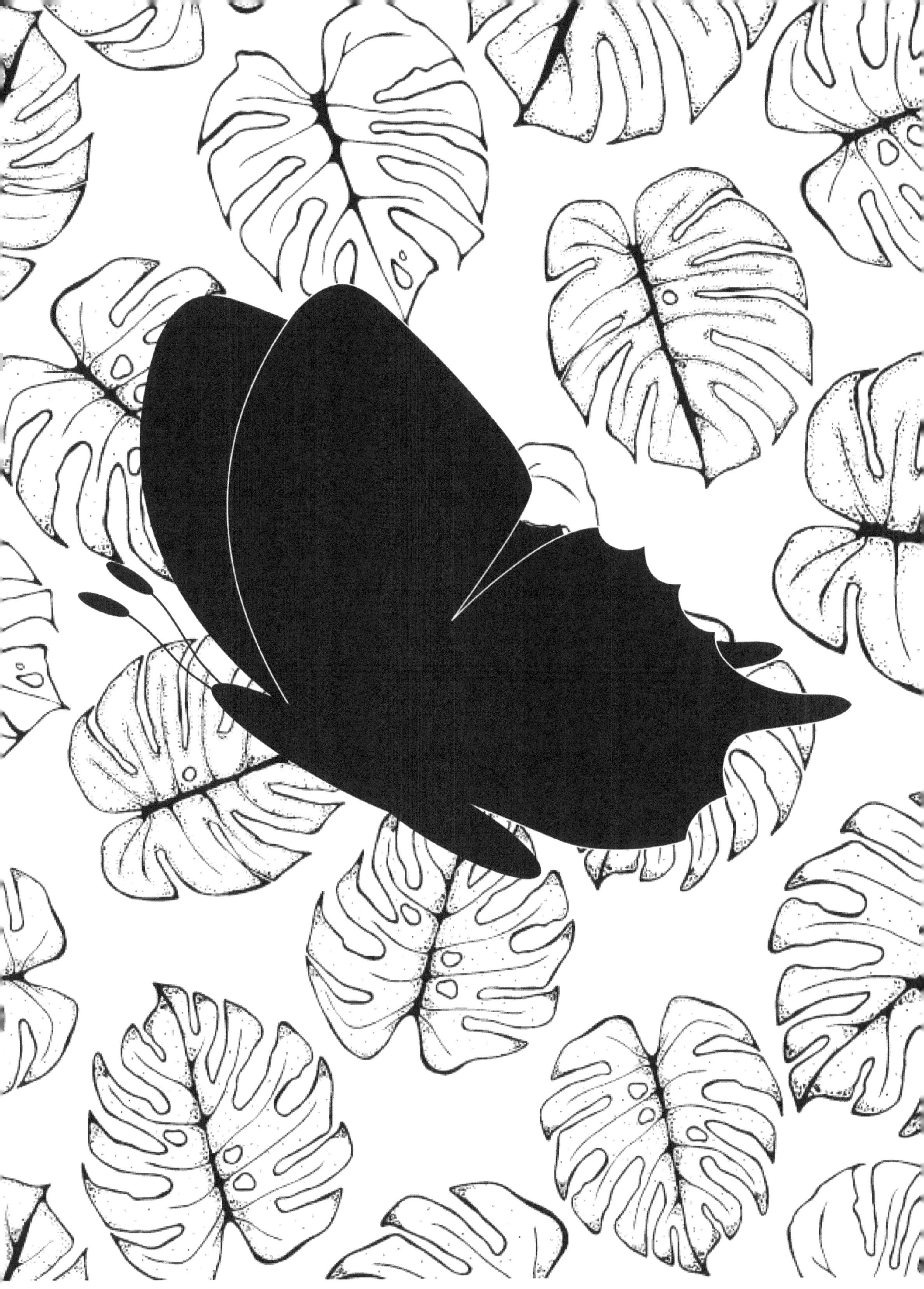

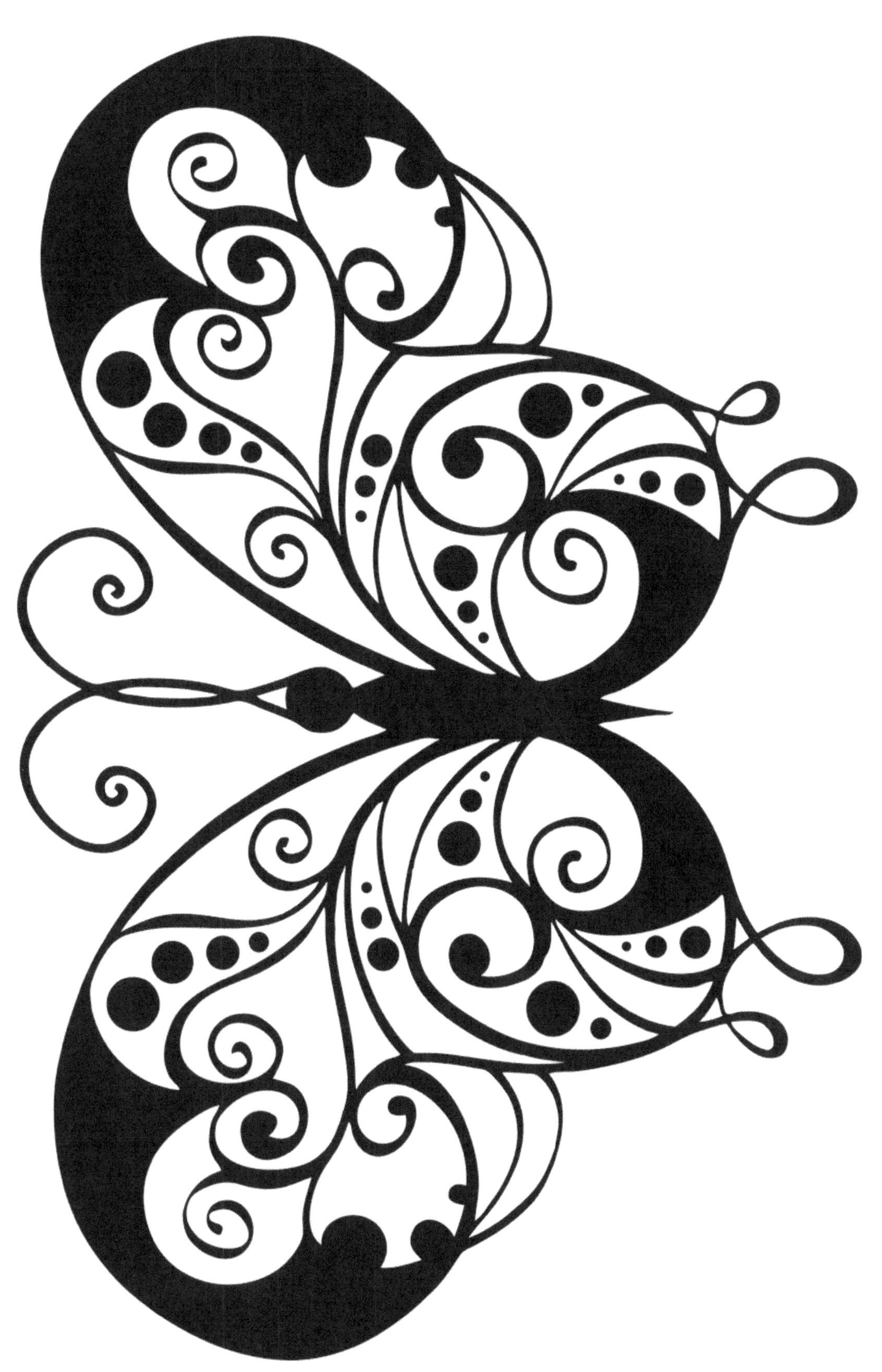

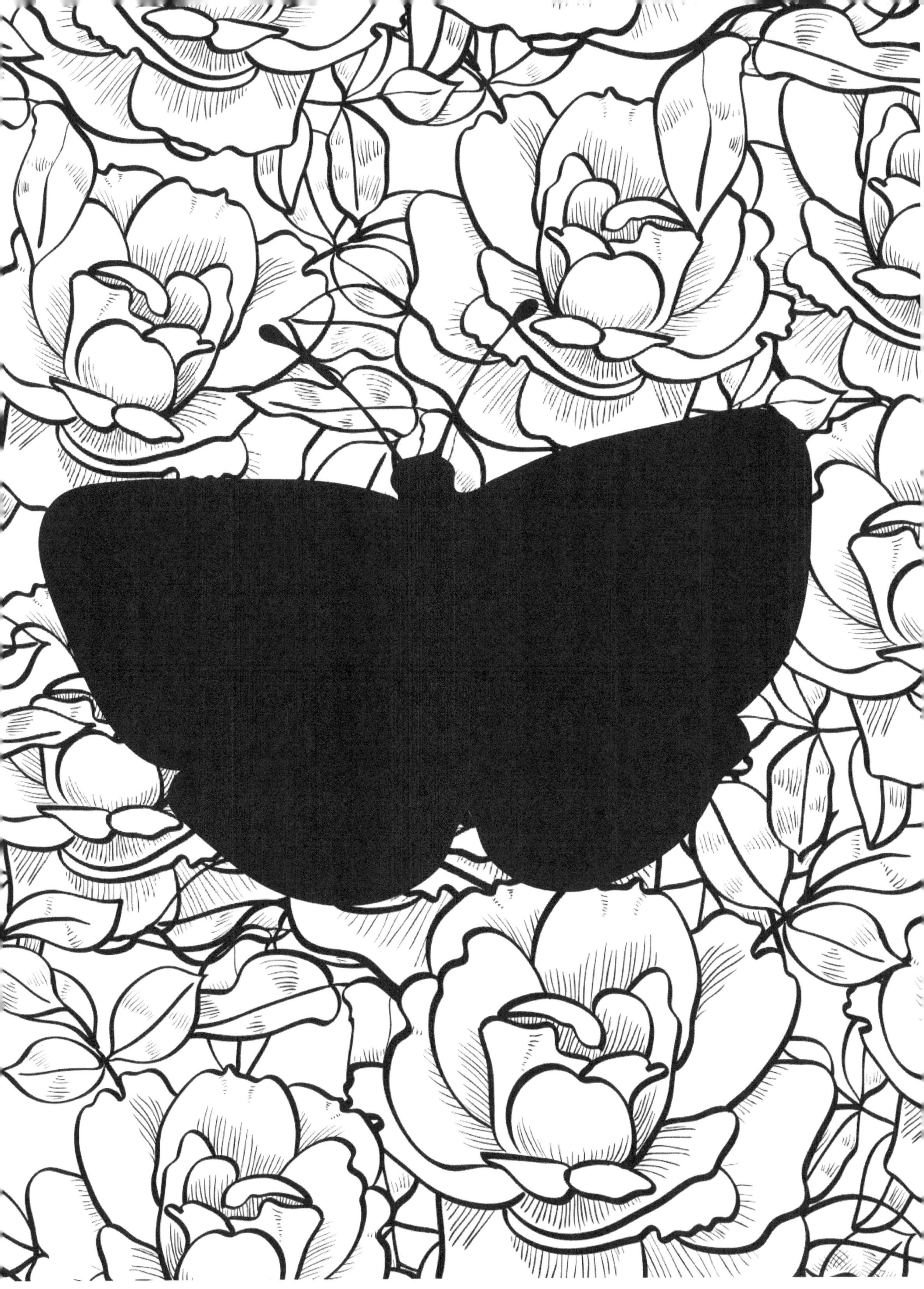

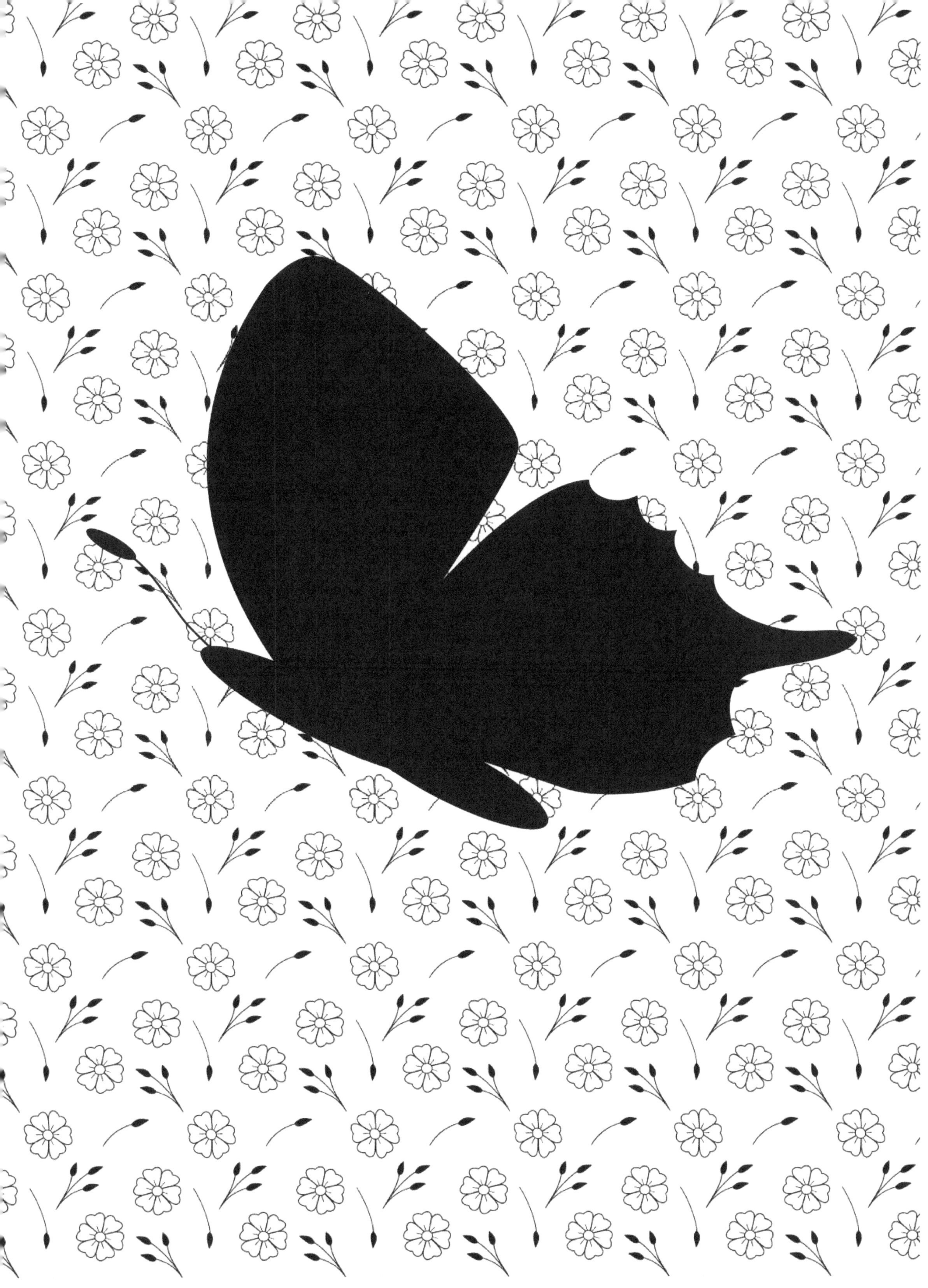

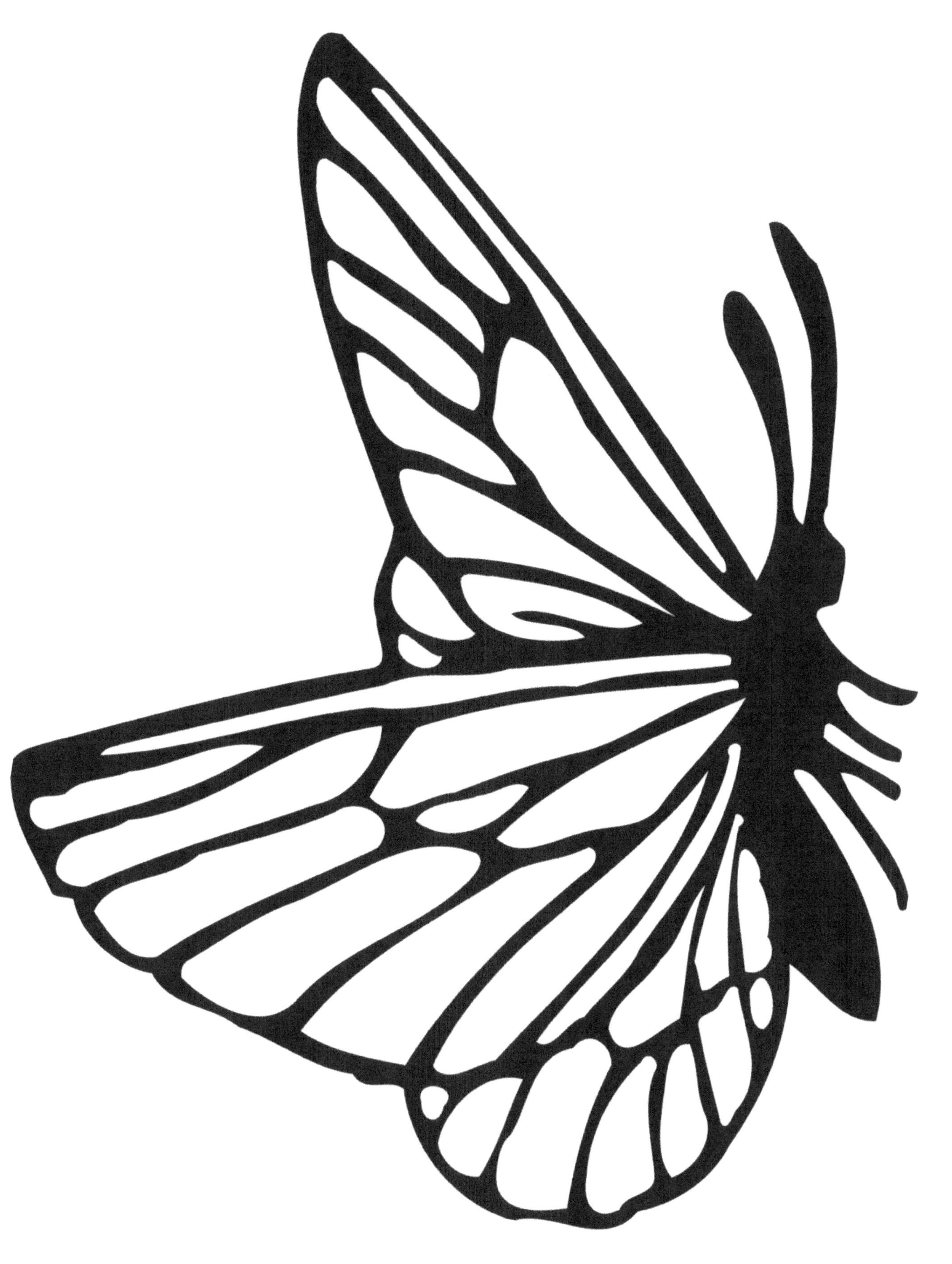

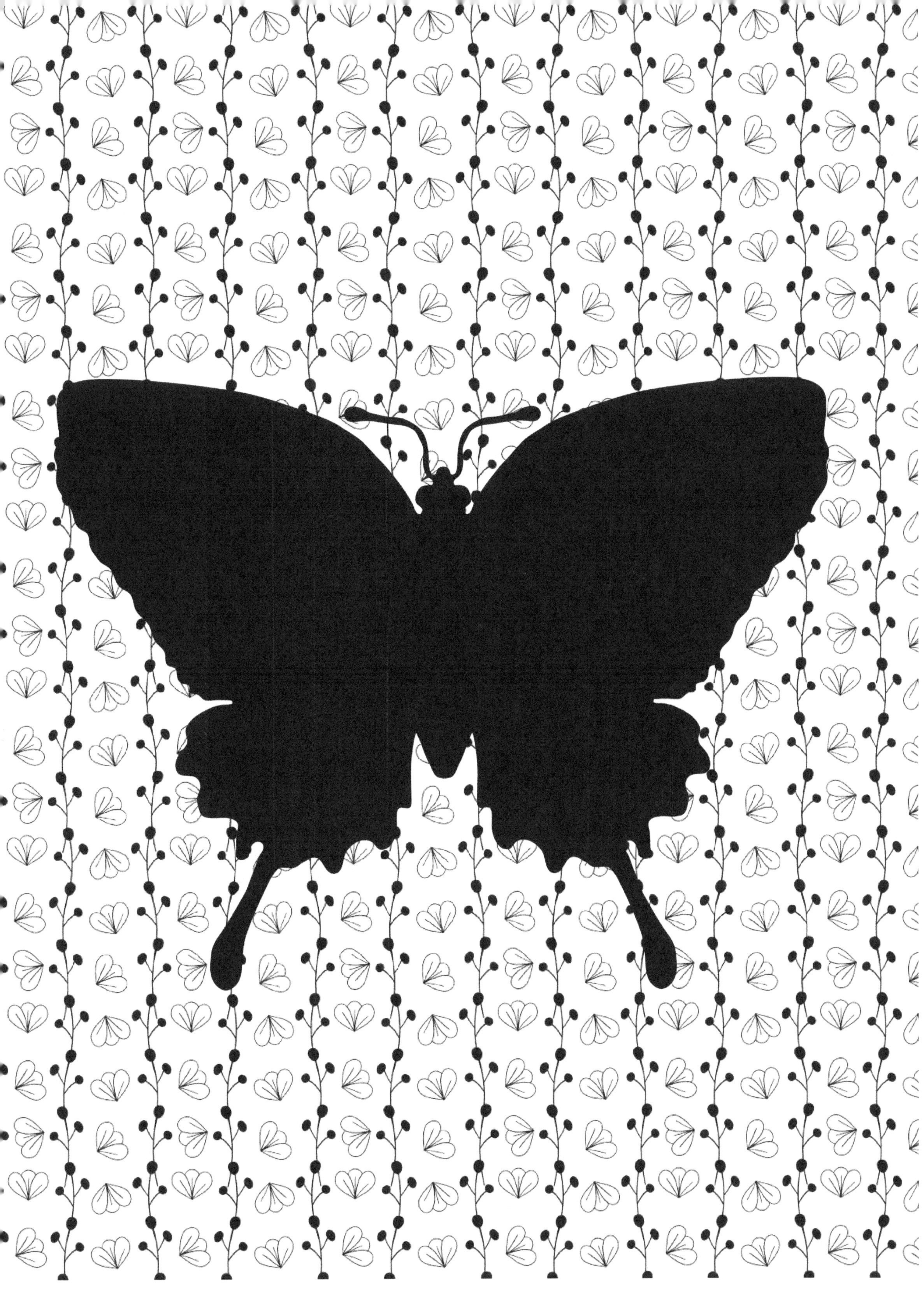

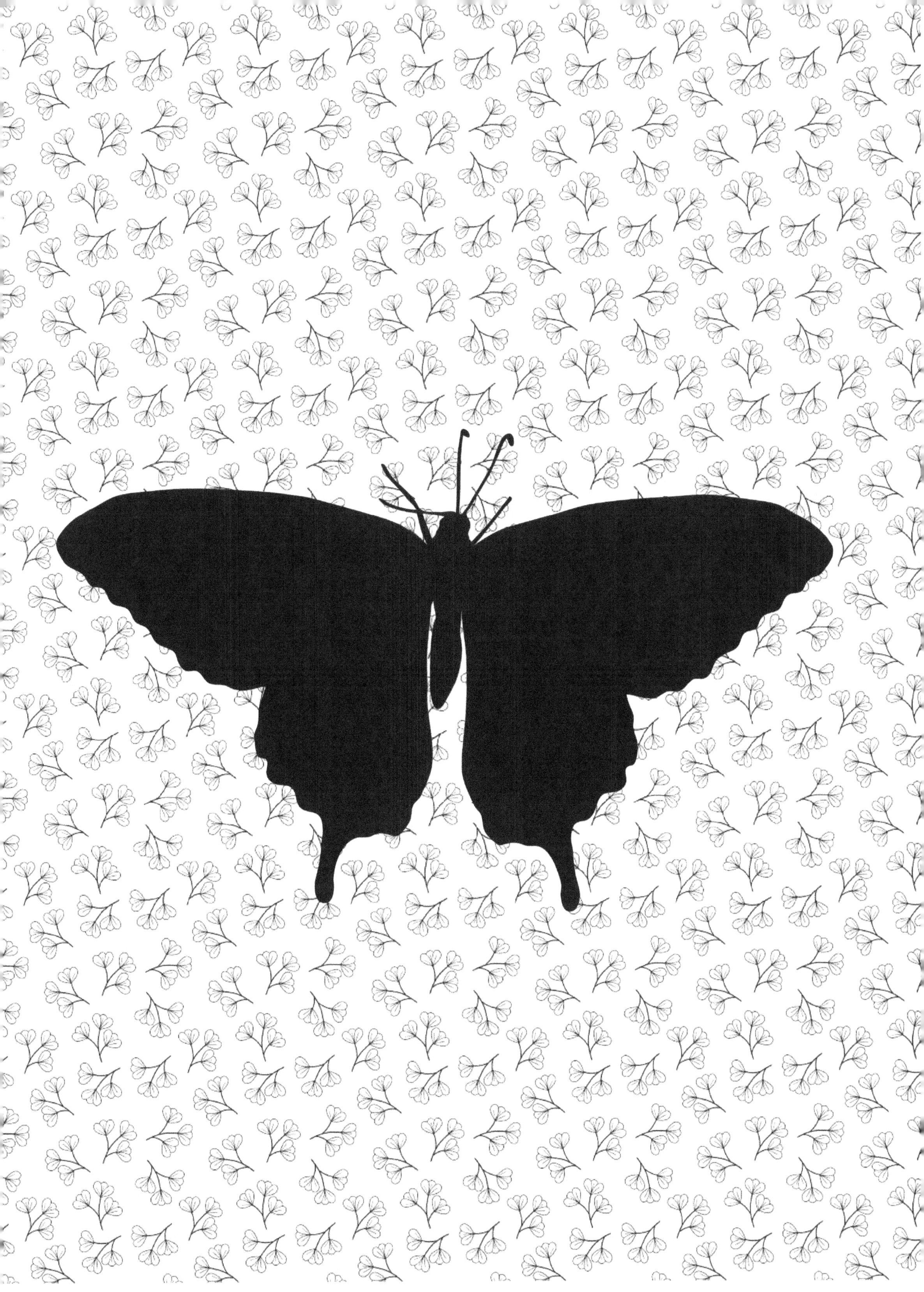

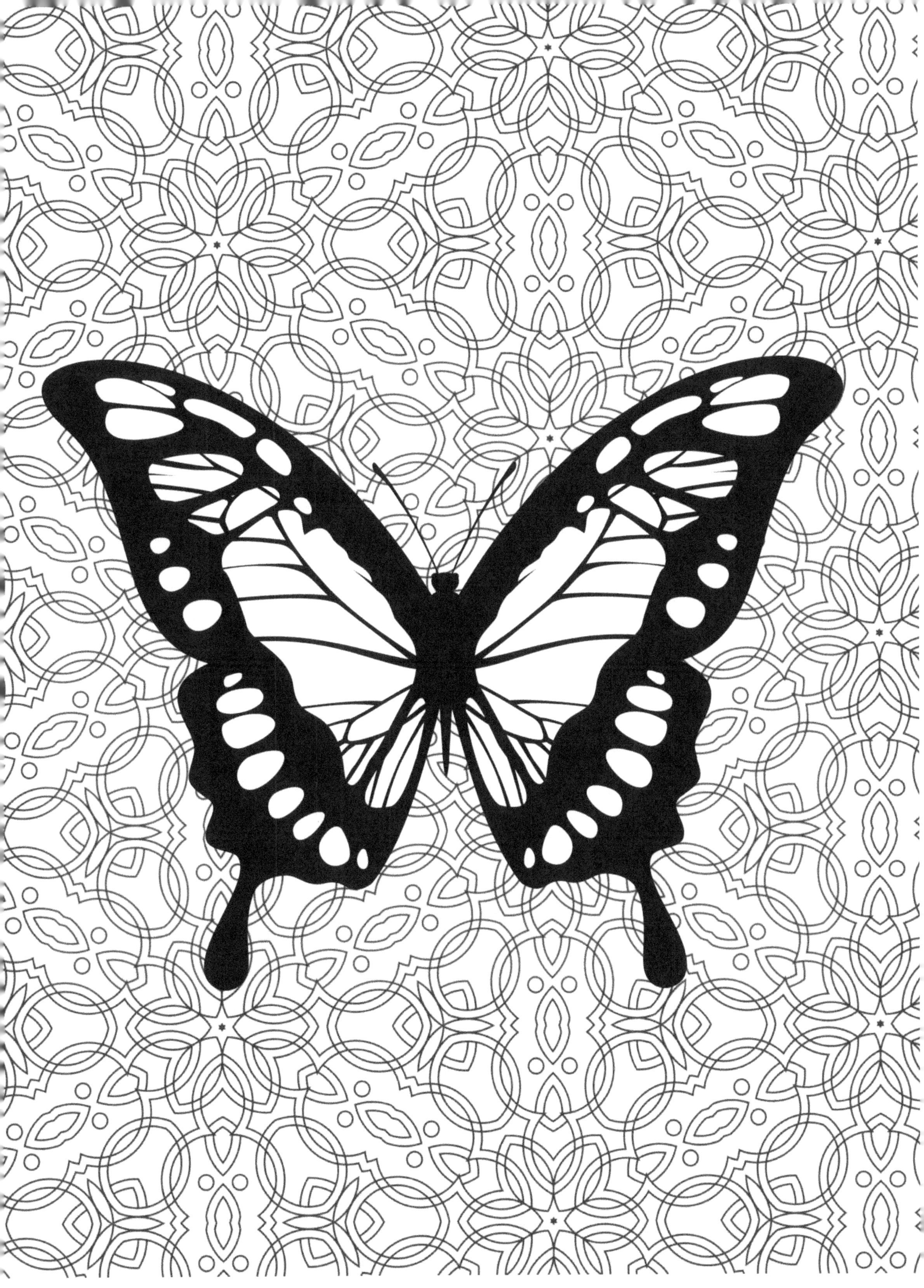

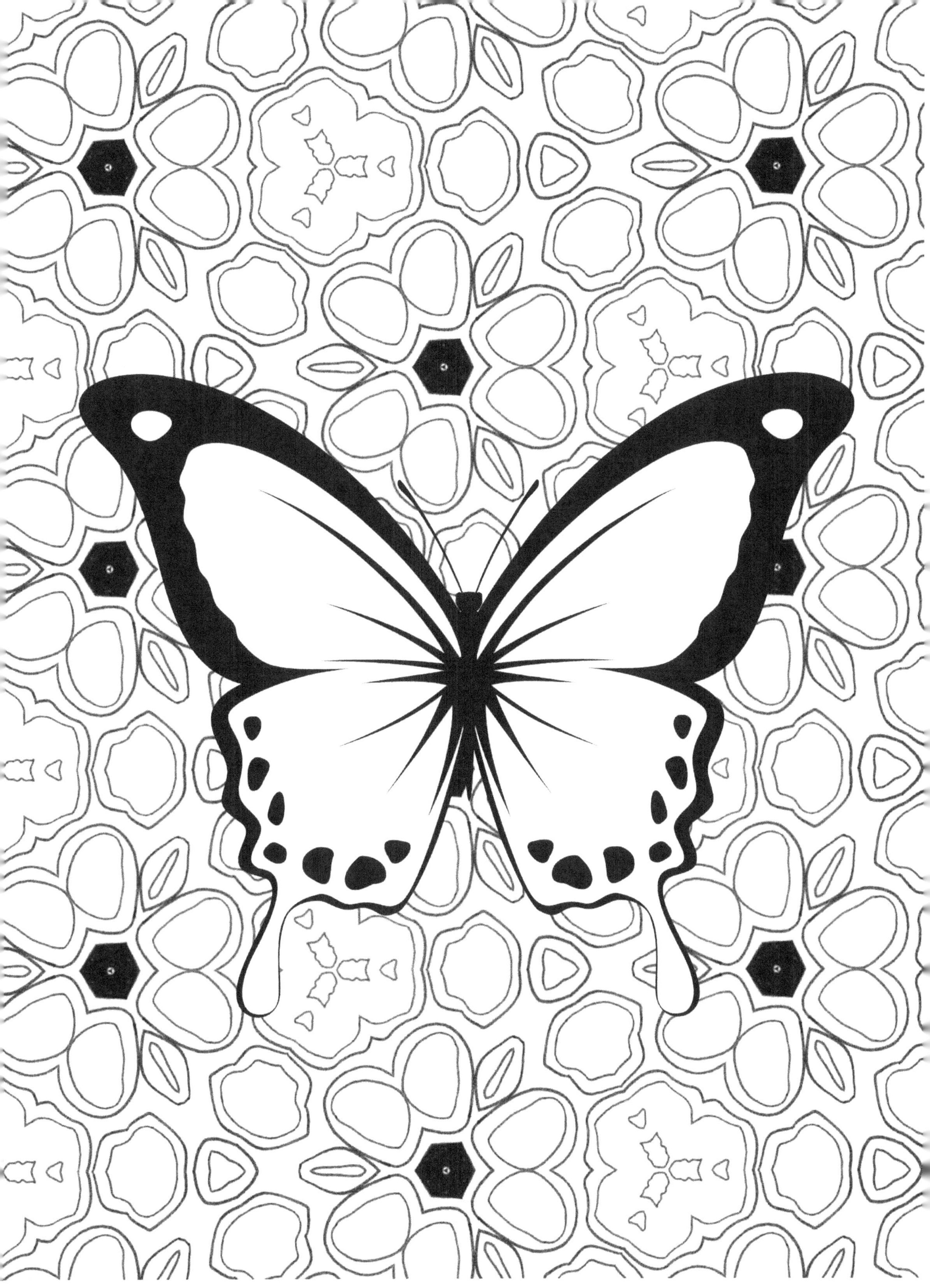

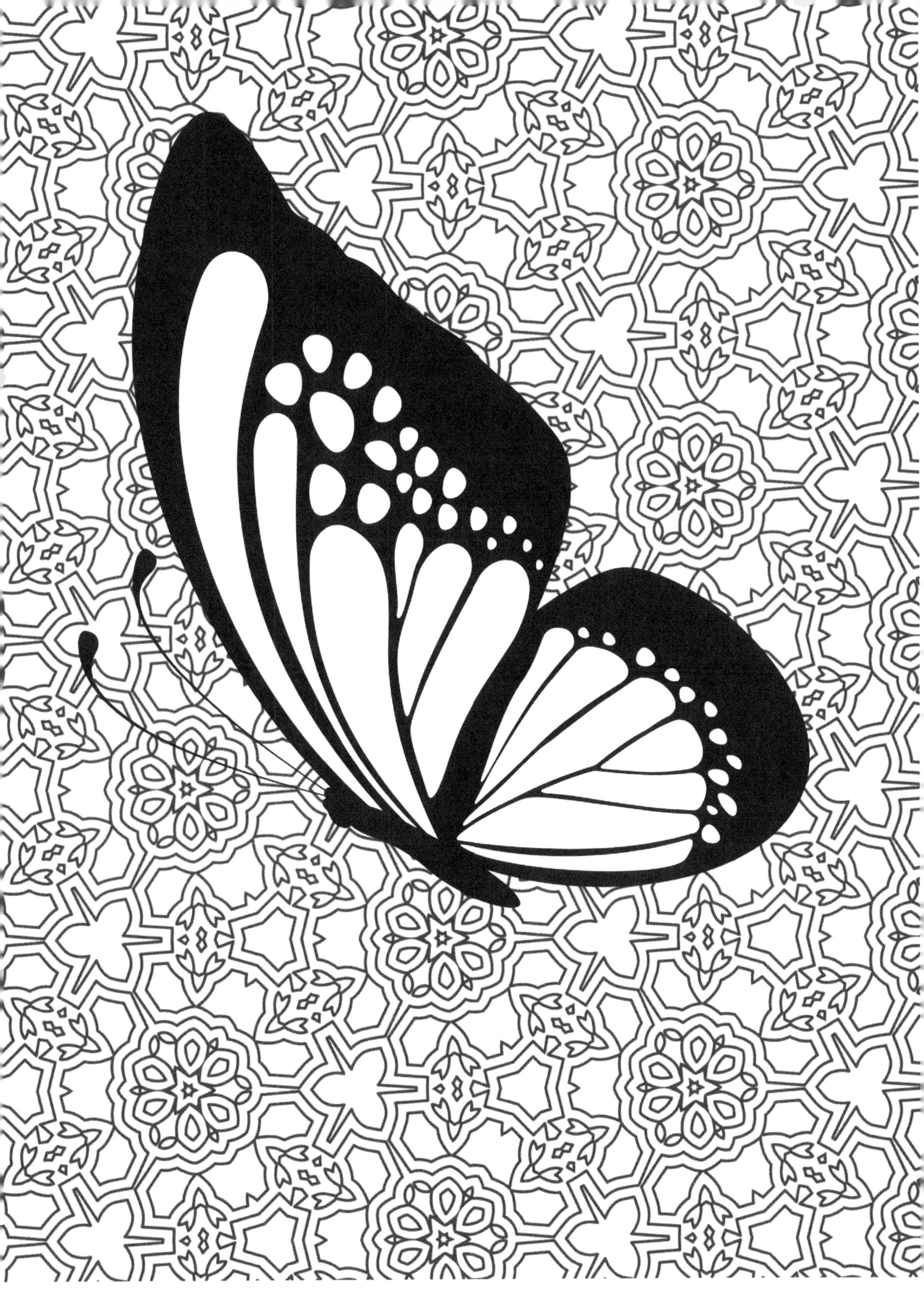

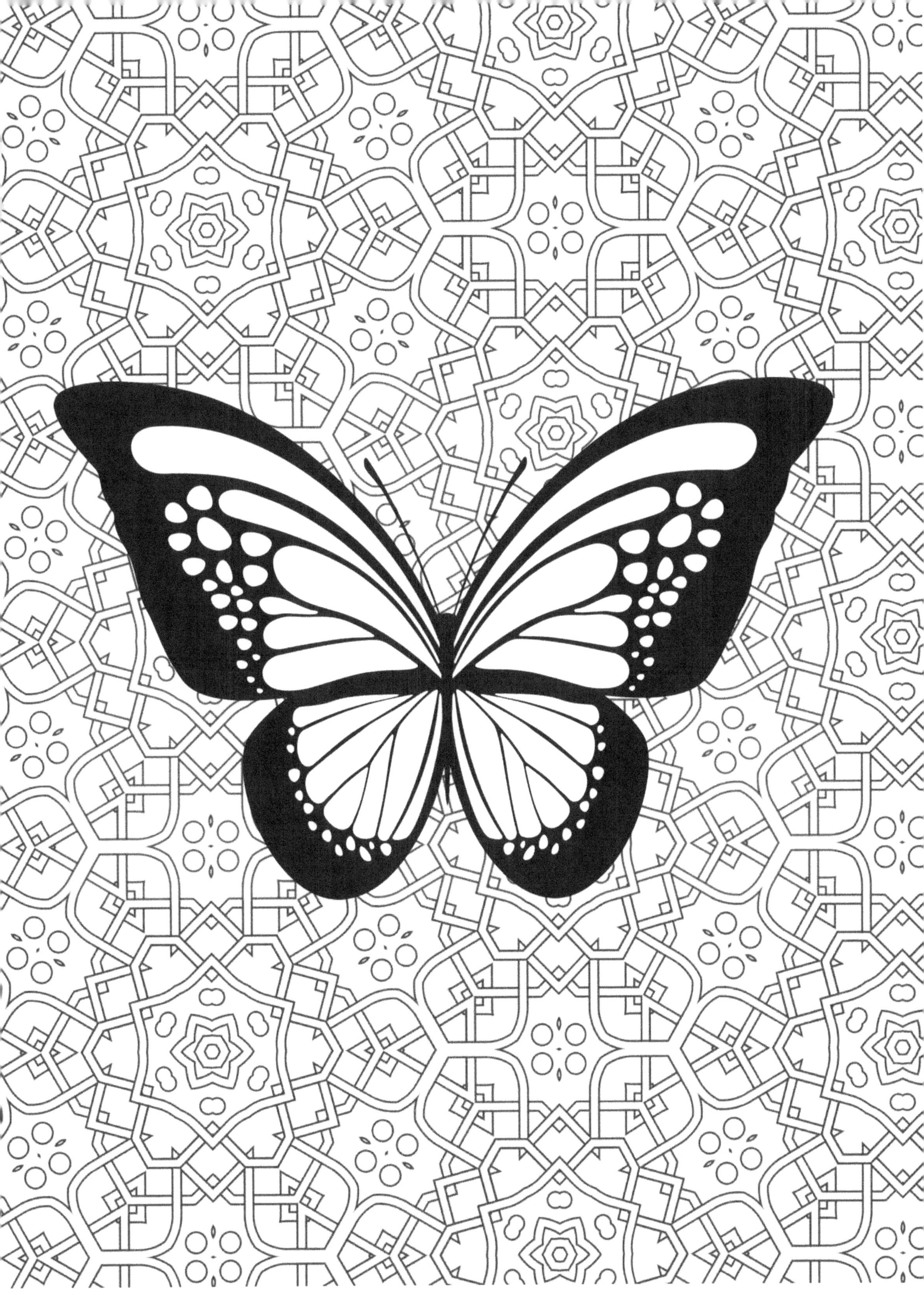

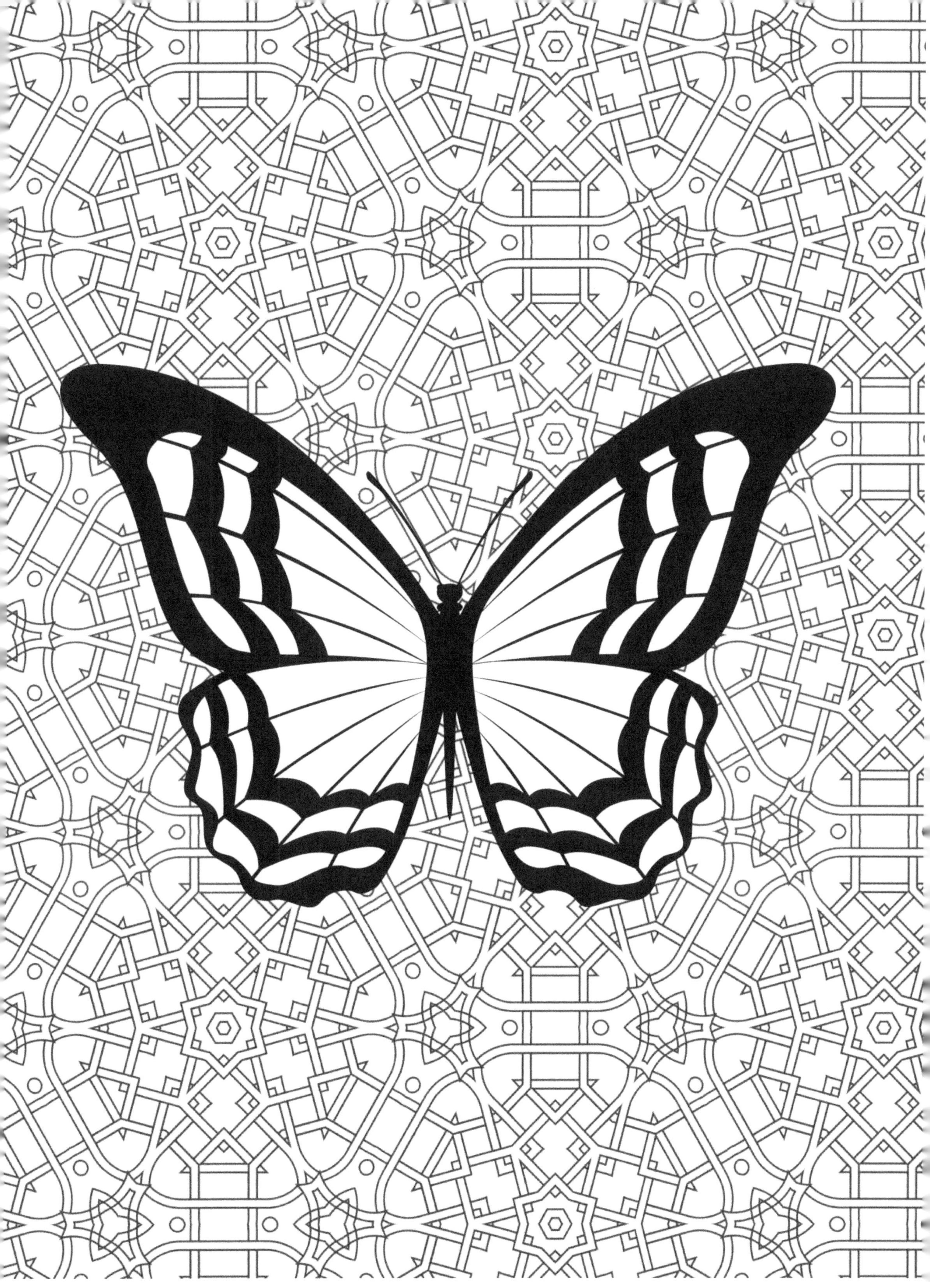

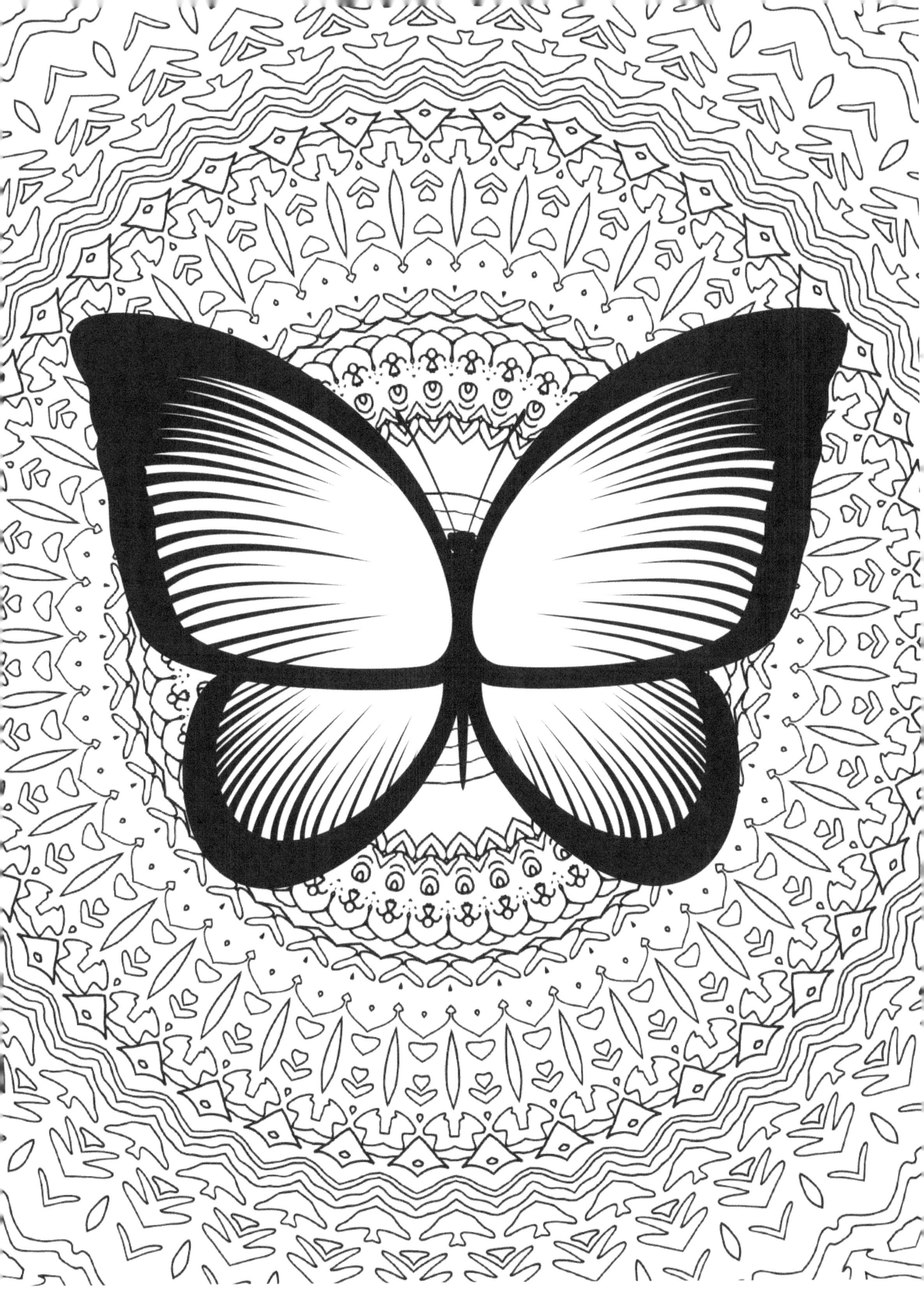

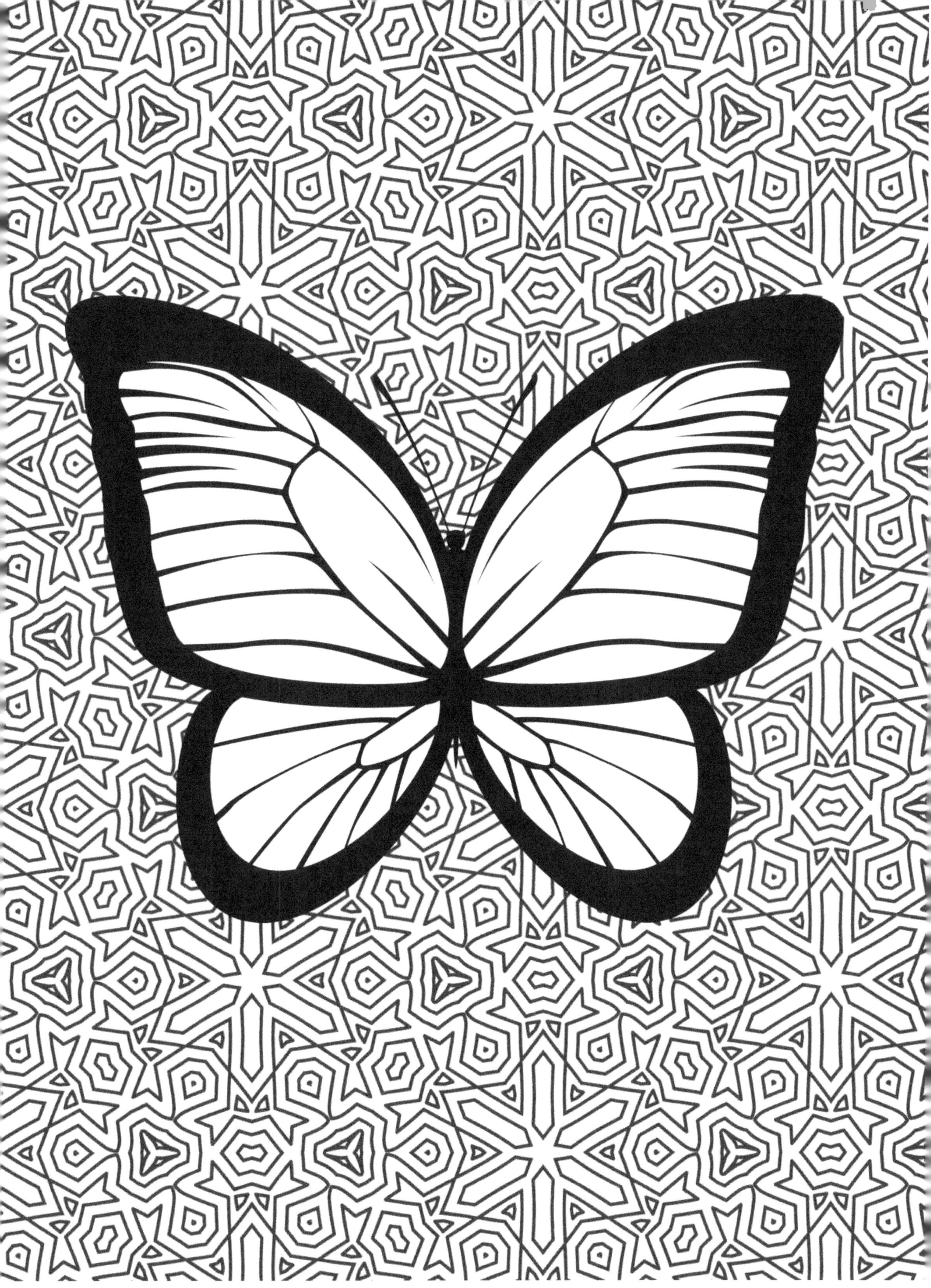

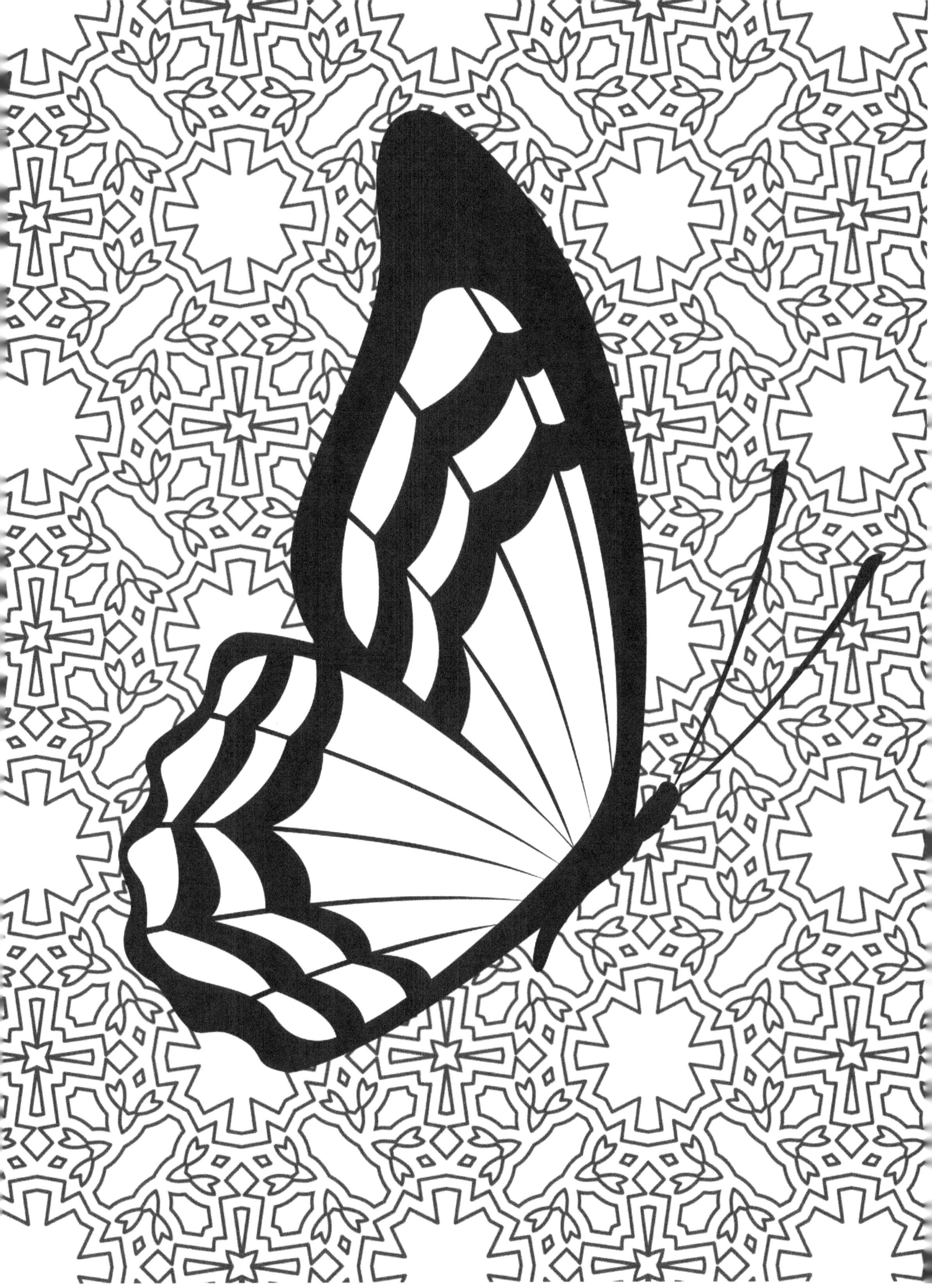

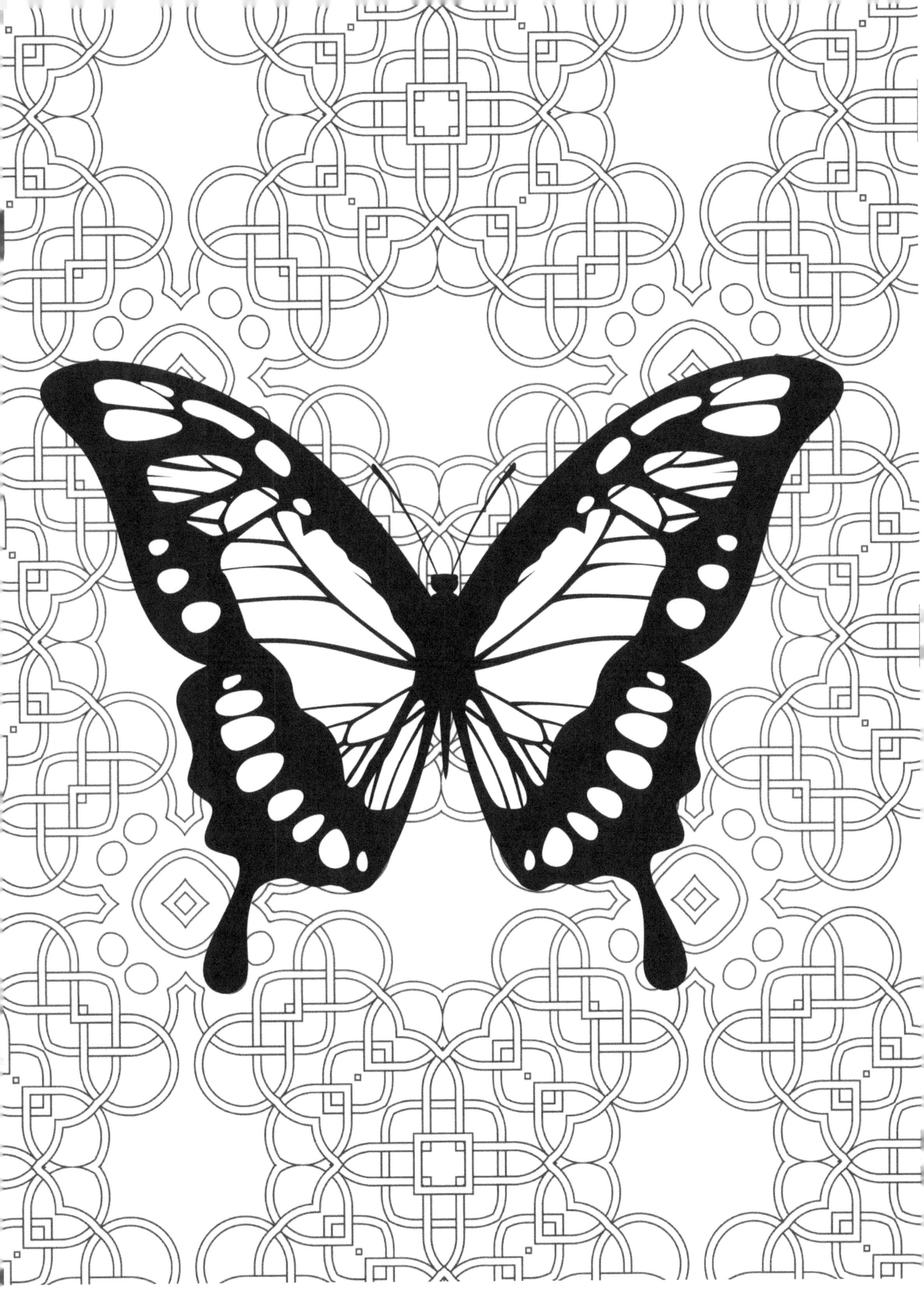

If you enjoyed this book, check out the coloring books available by

Sassy Scribblez

On Amazon.